IMPROVEMENT
OF
THE MIND

IMPROVEMENT
OF
THE MIND

by

Dr. Isaac Watts

Edited and Abridged
by
Stephen B. Helfant
J. David Coccoli

Helfant Publishing House
Groton, Massachusetts 01450

Library of Congress Catalog Card Number: 87-82282
ISBN 0-942969-00-6

Typeset at Crockergraphics
Needham, Massachusetts 02194

Printed in the United States by
Arcata Graphics/Halliday

TABLE OF CONTENTS

EDITORS' PREFACE

First published in 1741, Dr. Isaac Watts' *Improvement of the Mind* is a powerful treatise that deserves to be reintroduced for today's readers. Its message is as timeless and universal today as it was when first written. Though it received outstanding recommendations from many of the leading intellectuals of its time and was popular for a century thereafter, it then faded into obscurity for reasons that will be discussed later.

Dr. Isaac Watts (1674-1748) was an English philosopher, educator, author, essayist, lyricist, and poet of the 18th century who grew up in the era of enlightened self-interest, a school of philosophy originating principally with John Locke (1632-1704). In fact Dr. Watts' book is very much in the tradition of Locke. During the scientific revolution of the 17th and 18th centuries there was a clear necessity for a rational approach to the assimilation and evaluation of the bewildering multitude of observations, newly formulated theories, and contradictory speculations about the nature of the universe, man's place in it, and the role and objectives of education. Dr. Watts' book provides just such an approach. It contains extensive detailed discussions regarding the merits of direct observation, lectures, reading, conversation, and meditation as the five important methods of acquiring knowledge.

One of the great tributes to the effectiveness of Dr. Watts' treatise was the credit given it by one of the giants of 19th-century science, Michael Faraday. Although Faraday was an avid reader, he lacked proper schooling and at first had no criteria by which to judge the merit of the material he read. While working in a book shop, young Faraday first read *Improvement of the Mind*. Dr. Watts advised that a notebook be kept wherein all the observations and events of each day be noted and summarized. Faraday took up this practice and maintained it throughout his life. Dr. Watts recommended attendance at lectures, the exchange of letters with persons that have similar interests,[1] and participation in discussion groups. Faraday put all this to practice.[2]

Following Dr. Watts' rules and advice prepared Faraday to avoid the traps of imprecise language and hasty conclusions and no doubt was the basis for both the extreme care with which he chose his written words and the rigor he used in his experimental procedures. Faraday went on to originate the concepts that are the basis for the modern theory of electromagnetism. His descriptions of electric and magnetic fields of force and their interrelations were the observational material from which Maxwell was able to formulate his famous equations of electromagnetism. One might speculate that had Faraday not read *Improvement of the Mind* the course of science might well have been set back several decades.

Dr. Samuel Johnson[3] wrote of Dr. Watts: "He has provided instruction for all ages, from those who are lisping their first lessons, to the enlightened readers of Malbranche and Locke: ... he has taught the art of reasoning. ... Few books have been perused by me with greater pleasure than his *Improvement of the Mind*, of which the radical principles may indeed be found in Locke's *Conduct of the Understanding*; but they are so expanded and ramified by Watts, as to confer on him the merit of a work in the highest degree useful and pleasing. WHOEVER HAS THE CARE OF INSTRUCTING OTHERS, MAY BE CHARGED WITH DEFICIENCY IN HIS DUTY, IF THIS BOOK IS NOT RECOMMENDED."

The five methods of acquiring knowledge and their attendant rules presented by Dr. Watts appear to be matters of common sense. But in fact they only appear simple because of the effort that Dr. Watts expended to make them self-evident, both to challenge and guide receptive minds toward improvement. It is hoped that reintroduction of this material will help to counter some of the undesirable elements and

---

[1] In a discussion with a friend about epistolary correspondence Faraday stated: " ... the great Dr. Isaac Watts (great in all the methods respecting the attainment of learning) recommends it as a very effectual method of improving the mind of the person who writes and the person who receives." L. Pearce Williams, *Michael Faraday*, (New York: Basic Books, Inc., 1927), p. 21.

[2] *Ibid.*, pp. 10-13, 21, 46, 257.

[3] Dr. Samuel Johnson (1709-84) was regarded as one of the outstanding figures of 18th-century England. Among other achievements he was a poet, essayist, critic, journalist, lexicographer, and conversationalist.

habits of modern culture that tend toward destruction of rational thought.

As noted earlier, a variety of features in Dr. Watts' original text present a deterrent to its reintroduction for today's readers. These features have been eliminated in this abridged edition by the following changes:

- *Religion.* Dr. Watts devotes a great deal of space to theological and spiritual questions. This material has been deleted (indicated by "...") in the abridged version in the interest of brevity, and since it neither adds to nor detracts from the methods and rules.

- *Format.* Watts uses a free flowing style of text (i.e., lacking a hierarchy of indentations). The abridged version has been formatted using a hierarchy of indentations to clearly identify rules and subordinate information.

- *Examples.* Dr. Watts makes his points quite logically, but then often elaborates on them with numerous examples, some of which are written as parables — the substance of which may not be appealing to modern tastes. Material judged to be excessive and distracting has been deleted (indicated by "...") in the abridged version.

- *Vocabulary.* Dr. Watts occasionally uses words that are seldom encountered in modern literature (e.g., poesy) or the meaning of which is not attuned to contemporary usage (e.g., "science" is used to mean a body of knowledge rather than just the natural sciences). If the word is found in a comprehensive 20th-century dictionary it is retained; if not, then a substitution (indicated by *italic* type) is made which to the best of the editors' interpretation faithfully conveys the meaning intended by Dr. Watts.

The word "soul" is frequently used in this book, sometimes in the context of "mind" and other times to mean the "moral and emotional qualities of man."

The word "man" and other male-oriented terms are used frequently in this book. The reader should bear in mind that this book was written in the early 1700s with the prevailing attitudes of the time and presumably without any overt sexist intent. The editors considered liberalizing this abridged edition but decided that tampering with the sentence structure in this fashion might alter its meaning.

- *Major theme.* The major theme in each numbered section of the original is not clearly identified. To aid the reader in the abridged edition the pertinent words, which when combined form the theme, are printed in **bold** type. They are also listed in Appendix C, "Synopsis of the Chapters."

The spelling and grammar used by Dr. Watts have not been altered. Dr. Watts uses the word spellings of his day, such as "honour" instead of "honor", "shew" instead of "show" as a verb, and "practise" instead of "practice" as a verb. Because many of these spellings are still retained in modern England his spelling of words has not been altered. Dr. Watts makes extensive use of commas, colons, and semi-colons where modern taste would dictate separate sentences. Nevertheless, Dr. Watts' punctuation has been retained because tampering with the sentence structure might alter his intended meaning.

Introductory information, topic headings, and clarifications which have been added by the editors are printed in *italic* type.

If three dots (...), indicating a deletion, are located within a sentence, the sentence has been structured by the editors so that it can be read without pause.

Stephen B. Helfant and J. David Coccoli
January 1988

ACKNOWLEDGMENT

The idea of reintroducing the book, *Improvement of the Mind*, for the present generation was first conceived by Stephen Helfant in the 1960s while he was studying biographical material about the noted scientist Michael Faraday. It was Faraday's praise of the book that aroused Mr. Helfant's curiosity about the literary works of Dr. Watts. After reading *Improvement of the Mind*, Mr. Helfant became an avid proponent and the driving force behind the effort to issue a new edition of Dr. Watts' book.

J. David Coccoli, who has been associated with Mr. Helfant in editing and critiquing technical articles and books, contributed in great measure to this effort as co-editor.

Sponsorship for this project was provided by Gerald Gosselin. His unflagging enthusiasm was also a source of encouragement.

Linda Fava's dedicated efforts in critiquing the manuscript, typing, typesetting, and page preparation are gratefully acknowledged.

The cheerful efforts of Carol Lynde for typing are appreciated.

The support of David Crocker and the use of his typesetting and photographic facilities at *Crockergraphics* are appreciated.

The editors also wish to thank Roberta Crocker, Julius Feldman, Albert Freeman, David Keil, Martin Landey, Bradley Ross, Robert Var, and Dr. Robert Wilkinson for reviewing the manuscript.

Summary of type faces:

Normal = Text by Dr. Watts
Bold = Major theme by Dr. Watts
Italic = Supplemental text by editors
Bold Italic = Supplemental text by editors to major theme

INTRODUCTION

No man is obliged to learn and know every thing; this can neither be sought nor required, for it is utterly impossible: yet all persons are under some obligation to improve their own understanding; otherwise, it will be a barren desert, or a forest overgrown with weeds and brambles. Universal ignorance or infinite errors will overspread the mind which is utterly neglected and lies without any cultivation. ...

The common duties and benefits of society (which belong to every man living, as we are social creatures) and even our native and necessary relations to a family, a neighbourhood, or government, oblige all persons whatsoever to use their reasoning powers upon a thousand occasions; every hour of life calls for some regular exercise of our judgment, as to time and things, persons and actions. Without a prudent and discreet determination in matters before us, we shall be plunged into perpetual errors in our conduct. Now that which should always be practised, must at some time be learnt. ...

- Dr. Isaac Watts

Chapter 1

GENERAL RULES FOR IMPROVEMENT
OF KNOWLEDGE

*In this chapter Dr. Watts deals with motivational material, exhorting us
to admit our weaknesses in knowledge and reasoning power as the
necessary basis to generate enthusiasm for improving our minds.*

- Rules -

(1) **Deeply possess your mind with the vast importance of a good
judgment, and the rich and inestimable advantage of right
reasoning.** Review the instances of your own misconduct in life;
think seriously with yourselves how many follies and sorrows you
had escaped, and how much guilt and misery you had prevented,
if from your early years you had but taken due pains to judge aright
concerning persons, times, and things. This will awaken you with
lively vigour to address yourselves to the work of improving your
reasoning powers, and seizing every opportunity and advantage for
that end.

(2) **Consider the weaknesses, frailties, and mistakes of human nature
in general, which arise from the very constitution of a soul united
to an animal body,** and subjected to many inconveniences thereby.
... How much our powers of understanding are yet more
darkened, enfeebled, and imposed upon by our senses, our fancies,
and our unruly passions, etc. Consider the depth and difficulty of
many truths, and the flattering appearances of falsehood, whence
arises an infinite variety of dangers to which we are exposed in our
judgment of things. Read with greediness those authors that treat
of the doctrine of prejudices, prepossessions, and springs of error,

on purpose to make your soul watchful on all sides, that it suffer itself, as far as possible, to be imposed upon by none of them.

(3) A slight view of things so momentous is not sufficient. You should therefore **contrive and practise some proper methods to acquaint yourself with your own ignorance**, and to impress your mind with a deep and painful sense of the low and imperfect degrees of your present knowledge, that you may be incited with labour and activity to pursue after greater measures. Among others, you may find some such methods as these successful:

(a) **Take a wide survey now and then of the vast and unlimited regions of learning.** Let your meditations run over the names of all the sciences, with their numerous branchings, and innumerable particular themes of knowledge; and then reflect how few of them you are acquainted with in any tolerable degree. The most learned of mortals will never find occasion to act over again what is fabled of Alexander the Great, that when he had conquered what was called the eastern world, he wept for want of more worlds to conquer. The worlds of science are immense and endless.

(b) **Think what a numberless variety of questions and difficulties there are belonging even to that particular science in which you have made the greatest progress**, and how few of them there are in which you have arrived at a final and undoubted certainty; excepting only those questions in the pure and simple mathematics, whose theorems are demonstrable, and leave scarce any doubt; and yet, even in the pursuit of some few of these, mankind have been strangely bewildered.

(c) **Spend a few thoughts sometimes on** the **puzzling inquiries** concerning vacuums and atoms, the doctrine of infinites, indivisibles, and incommensurables in geometry, wherein there appear some insolvable difficulties: do this on purpose **to give you a more sensible impression of the poverty of your understanding and the imperfection of your knowledge.** This will teach you what a vain thing it is to fancy that you know all things, and will instruct you to think modestly of your present attainments, when every dust of the earth, and every inch of empty space, surmounts your understanding and

triumphs over your presumption. .... It is some good degree of improvement, when we are afraid to be positive.

(d) **Read the accounts of those vast treasures of knowledge which some of the dead have possessed, and some of the living do possess.** Read and be astonished at the almost incredible advances which have been made in science. Acquaint yourself with some persons of great learning, that by ... *conversation* among them, and comparing yourself with them, you may acquire a mean opinion of your own attainments, and may thereby be animated with new zeal, to equal them as far as possible, or to exceed; thus let your diligence be quickened by a generous and laudable emulation. ....

Remember this, that if upon some few superficial acquirements you value, exalt, and swell yourself, as though you were a man of learning already, you are thereby building a most unpassable barrier against all improvement; you will lie down and indulge idleness, and rest yourself contented in the midst of deep and shameful ignorance. ....

(4) **Presume not too much upon a bright genius, a ready wit, and good parts; for this, without labour and study, will never make a man of knowledge and wisdom.** This has been an unhappy temptation to persons of a vigorous and gay fancy, to despise learning and study. They have been acknowledged to shine in an assembly, and sparkle in a discourse on common topics, and thence they took it into their heads to abandon reading and labour, and grow old in ignorance; but when they had lost their vivacity of animal nature and youth, they became stupid and sottish even to contempt and ridicule. ....

The witty men sometimes have sense enough to know their own foible; and therefore they craftily shun the attacks of argument, or boldly pretend to despise and renounce them, because they are conscious of their own ignorance, and inwardly confess their want of acquaintance with the skill of reasoning.

(5) **As you are not to fancy yourself a learned man because you are blessed with a ready wit; so neither must you imagine that large and laborious reading, and a strong memory, can denominate you truly wise.** ....

It is meditation and studious thought, it is the exercise of your own reason and judgment upon all you read, that gives good sense even to the best genius, and affords your understanding the truest improvement. A boy of a strong memory may repeat a whole book of Euclid, yet be no geometrician; for he may not be able perhaps to demonstrate one single theorem. . . .

A well furnished library, and a capacious memory, are indeed of singular use toward the improvement of the mind; but if all your learning be nothing else but a mere amassment of what others have written, without a due penetration into the meaning, and without a judicious choice and determination of your own sentiments, I do not see what title your head has to true learning above your shelves. Though you have read philosophy and theology, morals and metaphysics in abundance, and every other art and science, yet if your memory is the only faculty employed, with the neglect of your reasoning powers, you can justly claim no higher character but that of a good historian of the sciences.

Here note, many of the foregoing advices are more peculiarly proper for those who are conceited of their abilities, and are ready to entertain a high opinion of themselves. But a modest, humble youth, of a good genius, should not suffer himself to be discouraged by any of these considerations. They are designed only as a spur to diligence, and a guard against vanity and pride.

(6) **Be not so weak as to imagine that a life of learning is a life of laziness and ease**; dare not give up yourself to any of the learned professions, unless you are resolved to labour hard at study, and can make it your delight, and the joy of your life. . . .

It is no idle thing to be a scholar indeed. A man much addicted to luxury and pleasure, recreation and pastime, should never pretend to devote himself entirely to the sciences, unless his soul be so reformed and refined, that he can taste all these entertainments eminently in his closet, among his books and papers. . . .

(7) **Let the hope of new discoveries, as well as the satisfaction and pleasure of known truths, animate your daily industry.** Do not think learning in general is arrived at its perfection, or that the knowledge of any particular subject in any science cannot be improved, merely because it has lain five hundred or a thousand

years without improvement. The present age, by ... the ingenuity and diligence of men, has brought to light such truths in natural philosophy, and such discoveries in the heavens and the earth, as seemed to be beyond the reach of man. But may there not be Sir Isaac Newtons in every science? You should never despair therefore of finding out that which has never yet been found, unless you see something in the nature of it which renders it unsearchable, and above the reach of our faculties. ...

(8) **Do not hover always on the surface of things,** nor take up suddenly with mere appearances; but penetrate into the depth of matters, as far as your time and circumstances allow, especially in those things which relate to your own profession. Do not indulge yourselves to judge of things by the first glimpse, or a short and superficial view of them; for this will fill the mind with errors and prejudices, ... give it a wrong turn and ill habit of thinking, and make much work for ... *retraction.* ...

As for those sciences, or those parts of knowledge, which either your profession, your leisure, your inclination, or your incapacity, forbid you to pursue with much application, or to search far into them, you must be contented with an historical and superficial knowledge of them, and not pretend to form any judgments of your own on those subjects which you understand very imperfectly.

(9) **Once a day, especially in the early years of life and study, call yourselves to an account what new ideas, what new proposition or truth you have gained, what further confirmation of known truths, and what advances you have made in any part of knowledge;** and let no day, if possible, pass away without some intellectual gain. Such a course, well pursued, must certainly advance us in useful knowledge. It is a wise proverb among the learned, "Let no day pass without one line at least." ... It was a sacred rule among the Pythagoreans, that they should every evening thrice run over the actions and affairs of the day, and examine what their conduct had been, what they had done, or what they had neglected. ... They assured their pupils that by this method they would make a noble progress in the path of virtue. ...

> Nor let soft slumber close your eyes,
> Before you've recollected thrice
> The train of action through the day:

Where have my feet chose out their way?
What have I learnt, where-e'er I've been,
From all I've heard, from all I've seen?
What know I more that's worth the knowing?
What have I done that's worth the doing?
What have I sought that I should shun?
What duty have I left undone?
Or into what new follies run? . . .

(10) **Maintain a constant watch at all times against a dogmatical spirit.**
Fix not your assent to any proposition in a firm and unalterable
manner, till you have some firm and unalterable ground for it, and
till you have arrived at some clear and sure evidence; till you have
turned the proposition on all sides, and searched the matter
through and through, so that you cannot be mistaken. And even
where you may think you have full grounds of assurance, be not
too early, nor too frequent, in expressing this assurance in too
peremptory and positive a manner, remembering that human
nature is always liable to mistake. . . . A dogmatical spirit has many
inconveniences attending it. . . . *For example:*

(a) **It stops the ear against all further reasoning upon that subject,
and shuts up the mind from all further improvements of
knowledge.** If you have resolutely fixed your opinion, though
it be upon too slight and insufficient grounds, yet you will
stand determined to renounce the strongest reason brought for
the contrary opinion, and grow obstinate against the force of
the clearest argument. . . .

(b) **A dogmatical spirit naturally leads us to arrogance of mind,
and gives a man some airs in conversation which are too
haughty and assuming.** . . .

A dogmatical spirit inclines a man to be censorious of his neighbours. Every one of his own opinions appears to him written as it
were with sunbeams; and he grows angry that his neighbour does
not see it in the same light. He is tempted to disdain his correspondents, as men of a low and dark understanding, because they
will not believe what he does. . . . These are the men that, when they
deal in controversy, delight in reproaches. They abound in tossing
about absurdity and stupidity among their brethren: they cast the
imputation of heresy and nonsense plentifully upon their antago-

nists; . . . A dogmatist in religion is not a great way off from a bigot, and is in high danger of growing up to be a bloody persecutor.

(11) **Though caution and slow assent will guard you against frequent mistakes and retractions; yet you should get humility and courage enough to retract any mistake, and confess an error**: frequent changes are tokens of levity in our first determinations; yet you should never be too proud to change your opinion, nor *afraid of being called* a changeling. . . . I confess it is better not to judge than judge falsely; it is wiser to withhold our assent till we see complete evidence; but if we have too suddenly given up our assent, as the wisest man does sometimes, *and* if we have professed what we find afterwards to be false, *then* we should never be ashamed nor afraid to renounce a mistake. . . .

(12) **He that would raise his judgment above the vulgar rank of mankind, and learn to pass a just sentence on persons and things, must take heed of a fanciful temper of mind, and a humorous conduct in his affairs.** Fancy and humour, early and constantly indulged, may expect an old age overrun with follies.

The notion of a humorist is one that is greatly pleased, or greatly displeased with little things; who sets his heart much upon matters of very small importance: who has his will determined every day by trifles, his actions seldom directed by the reason and nature of things, and his passions frequently raised by things of little moment. Where this practice is allowed, it will insensibly warp the judgment to pronounce little things great, and tempt you to lay a great weight upon them. In short, this temper will incline you to pass an unjust value on almost every thing that occurs; and every step you take in this path is just so far out of the way to wisdom.

(13) For the same reason **have a care of trifling with things important and momentous, or of sporting with things awful and sacred: do not indulge a spirit of ridicule**, as some witty men do on all occasions and subjects. This will as unhappily bias the judgment on the other side, and incline you to pass a low esteem on the most valuable objects. Whatsoever evil habit we indulge in practice, it will insensibly obtain a power over our understanding, and betray us into many errors. . . .

(14) **Ever maintain a virtuous and pious frame of spirit**: for an indulgence of vicious inclinations debases the understanding, and perverts the judgment. Whoredom and wine, and new wine, take away the heart and soul and reason of a man. Sensuality ruins the better faculties of the mind; an indulgence to appetite and passion enfeebles the powers of reason: it makes the judgment weak and susceptive of every falsehood, and especially of such mistakes as have a tendency towards the gratification of the animal; and it warps the soul aside strangely from that stedfast honesty and integrity that necessarily belongs to the pursuit of truth. It is the virtuous man who is in a fair way to wisdom. . . .

(15) **Watch against the pride of your own reason, and a vain conceit of your own intellectual powers.** . . .

Chapter 2

OBSERVATION, READING, INSTRUCTION BY LECTURES, CONVERSATION, AND STUDY, COMPARED

In this chapter Dr. Watts introduces the five methods for improving the mind and discusses their individual merits and the necessity of integrating all of them.

There are five eminent means or methods whereby the mind is improved in the knowledge of things, and these are observation, reading, instruction by lectures, conversation, and meditation (*study*); ...

- General Definitions -

Let us survey the general definitions or descriptions of them all.

(1) **Observation is the notice that we take of all occurrences** ... , whether they are sensible or intellectual, whether relating to persons or things, to ourselves or others. It is this that furnishes us, even from our infancy, with a rich variety of ideas and propositions, words and phrases: it is by this we know that fire will burn, that the sun gives light, that a horse eats grass, that an acorn produces an oak, that man is a being capable of reasoning and discourse, that our judgment is weak, that our mistakes are many, that our sorrows are great, that our bodies die and are carried to the grave, and that one generation succeeds another. All those things which we see, which we hear or feel, which we perceive by sense or consciousness, or which we know in a direct manner, with scarce any exercise of our reflecting faculties, or our reasoning powers, may be included under the general name of observation.

When this observation relates to any thing that immediately concerns ourselves, and of which we are conscious, it may be called experience. So I am said to know or experience that I have in myself a power of thinking, fearing, loving, etc., that I have appetites and passions working in me, and many personal occurrences have attended me in this life ...

When we are searching out the nature or properties of any being by various methods of trial, or when we apply some active powers, or set some causes to work to observe what effects they would produce, this sort of observation is called experiment. So when I throw a bullet into water, I find it sinks; and when I throw the same bullet into quicksilver, I see it swims: but if I beat out this bullet into a thin hollow shape, like a dish, then it will swim in the water too. So when I strike two flints together, I find they produce fire: when I throw a seed into the earth, it grows up into a plant.

All these belong to the first method of knowledge: which I shall call observation.

(2) **Reading is that means or method of knowledge whereby we acquaint ourselves with what other men have written,** or published to the world in their writings. These arts of reading and writing are of infinite advantage; for by them we are made partakers of the sentiments, observations, reasonings, and improvements of all the learned world, in the most remote nations, and in former ages almost from the beginning of mankind.

(3) **Public or private lectures are such verbal instructions as are given by a teacher** while the learners attend in silence. This is the way of learning ... philosophy ... from the professor's chair; or of mathematics, by a teacher shewing us various theorems or problems, i.e., speculations or practices by demonstration and operation, with all the instruments of art necessary to those operations.

(4) **Conversation is another method of improving our minds, wherein, by mutual discourse and inquiry, we learn the sentiments of others,** as well as communicate our sentiments to others in the same manner. Sometimes indeed, though both parties speak by turns, yet the advantage is only on one side, as when a teacher and a learner meet and discourse together: but frequently the profit is mutual.

Under this head of conversation we may also rank disputes of various kinds.

(5) **Meditation or study includes all those exercises of the mind, whereby we render all the former methods useful** for our increase in true knowledge and wisdom. It is by meditation we come to confirm our memory of things that pass through our thoughts in the occurrences of life, in our own experiences, and in the observations we make. It is by meditation that we draw various inferences, and establish in our minds general principles of knowledge. It is by meditation that we compare the various ideas which we derive from our senses, or from the operations of our souls, and join them in propositions. It is by meditation that we fix in our memory whatsoever we learn, and form our own judgment of the truth or falsehood, the strength or weakness, of what others speak or write. It is meditation ... that draws out long chains of argument, and searches or finds deep and difficult truths which before lay concealed in darkness.

It would be a needless thing to prove, that our own solitary meditations, together with the few observations that the most part of mankind are capable of making, are not sufficient, of themselves, to lead us into the attainment of any considerable proportion of knowledge, at least in an age so much improved as ours is, without the assistance of conversation and reading, and other proper instructions that are to be attained in our days. Yet each of these five methods have their peculiar advantages, whereby they assist each other; and their peculiar defects which have need to be supplied by the other's assistance. Let us trace over some of the particular advantages of each.

- Advantages of Each Method -

(1) ... **Observation** ...

(a) It is owing to observation that our mind is furnished with the **first simple and complex ideas**. It is this *that* lays the groundwork and foundation of all knowledge, and makes us capable of using any of the other methods of improving the mind: for if we did not attain a variety of sensible and intellectual ideas by the sensations of outward objects, by the consciousness of our own appetites and passions, pleasures and pains, and by inward experience of the actings of our own

spirits, it would be impossible either for men or books to teach us any thing. It is observation that must give us our first ideas of things as it includes in it sense and consciousness.

(b) All our knowledge derived from observation, whether it be of single ideas or of propositions, is **knowledge gotten at first hand.** Hereby we see and know things as they are, or as they appear to us; we take the impressions of them on our minds from the original objects themselves, which give a clearer and stronger conception of things: these ideas are more lively, and the propositions (at least in many cases) are much more evident. Whereas, what knowledge we derive from lectures, reading, and conversation, is but the copy of other men's ideas, that is, the picture of a picture; and it is one removed further from the original.

(c) Another advantage of observation is, that we may **gain knowledge all the day long**, and every moment of our lives; and every moment of our existences we may be adding something to our intellectual treasures ... , except only while we are asleep, and even then the remembrance of our dreaming will teach us some truths, and lay a foundation for a better acquaintance with human nature, both in the powers and in the frailties of it.

(2) ... **Reading** ...

(a) By reading **we acquaint ourselves,** in a very extensive manner, **with the affairs, actions, and thoughts of the living and the dead**, in the most remote nations, and most distant ages, and that with as much ease as though they lived in our own age and nation. By reading of books we may learn something from all parts of mankind; whereas by observation we learn all from ourselves, and only what comes within our own direct cognizance. By conversation we can only enjoy the assistance of a few persons, viz., those who are near us, and live at the same time when we do, that is, our neighbours and contemporaries; but our knowledge is much more narrowed still, if we confine ourselves merely to our own solitary reasonings, without much observation or reading: for then all our improvement must arise only from our own inward powers and meditations.

(b) By reading we learn not only the actions and the sentiments of different nations and ages, but **we transfer to ourselves** the knowledge and improvements of the most learned men, the wisest and the best of mankind, when or wheresoever they lived: for though many books have been written by weak and injudicious persons, yet the most of those books which have obtained great reputation in the world are **the products of great and wise men in their several ages and nations**: whereas we can obtain the conversation and instruction of those only who are within the reach of our dwelling, or our acquaintance, whether they are wise or unwise: and sometimes that narrow sphere scarce affords any person of great eminence in wisdom or learning, unless our instructors happen to have this character. And as for our own ... meditations, even when we arrive at some good degrees of learning, our advantage for further improvement in knowledge by them is still far more contracted than what we may derive from reading.

(c) When we read good authors, **we learn the best, the most laboured, and most refined sentiments**, even of those wise and learned men; for they have studied hard, and have committed to writing their maturest thoughts, and the result of their long study and experience: whereas by conversation, and in some lectures, we obtain many times only the present thoughts of our tutors and friends, which (though they may be bright and useful) yet, at first perhaps, may be sudden and indigested, and are mere hints which have risen to no maturity.

(d) It is another advantage of reading, that **we may review what we have read**; we may consult the page again and again, and meditate on it, at successive seasons, in our serenest and retired hours, having the book always at hand: but what we obtain by conversation and in lectures, is oftentimes lost again as soon as the company breaks up, or at least when the day vanishes, unless we happen to have the talent of a good memory, or quickly retire and note down what remarkables we have found in those discourses. And for the same reason, and for the want of retiring and writing, many a learned man has lost several useful meditations of his own, and could never recall them again.

(3) ... **Lectures** ...

(a) There is something more sprightly, **more delightful and entertaining** in the living discourse of a wise, learned, and well-qualified teacher **than** there is in the silent and sedentary practice of **reading**. The very turn of voice, the good pronunciation, and the polite and alluring manner which some teachers have attained, will engage the attention, keep the soul fixed, and convey and insinuate into the mind the ideas of things in a more lively and forcible way than the mere reading of books in the silence and retirement of the closet.

(b) **A tutor or instructor, when he paraphrases and explains other authors, can mark out the precise point of difficulty or controversy,** and unfold it. He can shew you which paragraphs are of greatest importance, and which are of less moment. He can teach his hearers what authors, or what parts of an author, are best worth reading on any particular subject, and thus save his disciples much time and pains, by shortening the labours of their closet and private studies. He can shew you what were the doctrines of the ancients, in a compendium which perhaps would cost much labour and the perusal of many books to attain. He can inform you what new doctrines or sentiments are arising in the world before they come to be public; as well as acquaint you with his own private thoughts, and his own experiments and observations, which never were, and perhaps never will be, published to the world, and yet may be very valuable and useful.

(c) A living instructor **can convey to our senses those notions** with which he would furnish our minds, when he teaches us natural philosophy, or most parts of mathematical learning. He can make the experiments before our eyes. He can describe figures and diagrams, point to the lines and angles, and make out the demonstration in a more intelligible manner by sensible means, **which cannot so well be done by mere reading**, even though we should have the same figures lying in a book before our eyes. A living teacher, therefore, is a most necessary help in these studies.

I might add also, that even where the subject of discourse is moral, logical, or rhetorical, etc., and which does not directly come under the notice of our senses, a tutor may explain his ideas by such familiar examples, and plain or simple similitudes, as seldom find place in books and writings.

(d) When an instructor in his lectures delivers any matter of difficulty, or expresses himself in such a manner as seems obscure, so that you do not take up his ideas clearly or fully, you **have opportunity**, at least when the lecture is finished, or at other proper seasons, **to inquire how** such a sentence should be understood, or how such **a difficulty may be explained and removed.**

If there be permission given to free converse with the tutor, either in the midst of the lecture, or rather at the end of it, concerning any doubts or difficulties that occur to the hearer, this brings it very near to conversation or discourse.

(4) ... **Conversation** ...

(a) **When we converse familiarly with a learned friend, we have his own help at hand to explain to us** every word and sentiment that seems obscure in his discourse, and to inform us of his whole meaning; so that we are in much less danger of mistaking his sense: whereas in books, whatsoever is really obscure may also abide always obscure without remedy, since the author is not at hand, that we may inquire his sense. ...

(b) When we are discoursing upon any theme with a friend, **we may propose our doubts and objections** against his sentiments, **and have them solved and answered at once.** The difficulties that arise in our minds may be removed by one enlightening word of our correspondent; whereas in reading, if a difficulty or question arise in our thoughts, which the author has not happened to mention, we must be content without a present answer or solution of it. Books cannot speak.

(c) Not only the doubts which arise in the mind upon any subject of discourse are easily proposed and solved in conversation, but the very **difficulties we meet with in books, and in our private studies, may find a relief by friendly conference.** We may pore upon a knotty point in solitary meditation many

months without a solution, because perhaps we have gotten into a wrong tract of thought; and our labour (while we are pursuing a false scent) is not only useless and unsuccessful, but it leads us perhaps into a long train of error for want of being corrected in the first step. But if we note down this difficulty when we read it, we may propose it to an ingenious correspondent when we see him; we may be relieved in a moment, and find the difficulty vanish: he beholds the object perhaps in a different view, sets it before us in quite another light, leads us at once into evidence and truth, and that with a delightful surprise.

(d) Conversation **calls out into light what has been lodged in all the recesses and secret chambers of the soul:** by occasional hints and incidents it brings old useful notions into remembrance; it unfolds and displays the hidden treasures of knowledge with which reading, observation, and study had before furnished the mind. By mutual discourse, the soul is awakened and allured to bring forth its hoards of knowledge, and it learns how to render them most useful to mankind. A man of vast reading without conversation, is like a miser, who lives only to himself.

(e) In free and friendly conversation, our **intellectual powers are more animated**, and our spirits act with superior vigour in the quest and pursuit of unknown truths. There is a sharpness and sagacity of thought that attends conversation, beyond what we find whilst we are shut up reading and musing in our retirements. Our souls may be serene in solitude, but not sparkling, though perhaps we are employed in reading the works of the brightest writers. Often has it happened in free discourse, that new thoughts are strangely struck out, and the seeds of truth sparkle and blaze through the company, which in calm and silent reading would never have been excited. By conversation you will both give and receive this benefit; as flints, when put into motion, and striking against each other, produce living fire on both sides, which would never have arisen from the same hard materials in a state of rest.

(f) In generous conversation, amongst ingenious and learned men, **we have a great advantage of proposing our private**

opinions, and of bringing our own sentiments to the test, and learning in a more compendious and safer way what the world will judge of them, how mankind will receive them, what objections may be raised against them, what defects there are in our scheme, and how to correct our own mistakes; which advantages are not so easy to be obtained by our own private meditations: for the pleasure we take in our own notions, and the passion of self-love, as well as the narrowness of our views, tempt us to pass too favourable an opinion on our own schemes; whereas the variety of genius in our several associates, will give happy notices how our opinions will stand in the view of mankind.

(g) It is also another considerable advantage of conversation, that it **furnishes the student with the knowledge of men and the affairs of life**, as reading furnishes him with book learning. A man who dwells all his days among books, may have amassed together a vast heap of notions; but he may be a mere scholar, which is a contemptible sort of character in the world. A hermit, who has been shut up in his cell in a college, has contracted a sort of mould and rust upon his soul, and all his airs of behaviour have a certain awkwardness in them; but these awkward airs are worn away by degrees in company: the rust and the mould are filed and brushed off by polite conversation. The scholar now becomes a citizen or a gentleman, a neighbour and a friend; he learns how to dress his sentiments in the fairest colours, as well as to set them in the strongest light. Thus he brings out his notions with honour; he makes some use of them in the world, and improves the theory by the practice.

But before we proceed too far in finishing a bright character by conversation, we should consider that something else is necessary besides an acquaintance with men and books: and therefore I add the next method.

(5) ... **Meditation or study** ... Mere *observation*, lectures, reading, and conversation, without thinking, are not sufficient to make a man of knowledge and wisdom. It is our thought and reflection, study and meditation, *that* must attend all the other methods of improvement, and perfect them. It carries these advantages with it:

(a) Though observation and instruction, reading and conversation, may furnish us with many ideas of men and things, yet it is **our own meditation, and the labour of our own thoughts**, that must **form our judgment of things.** Our own thoughts should join or disjoin these ideas in a proposition for ourselves: it is our own mind that must judge for ourselves concerning the agreement or disagreement of ideas, and form propositions of truth out of them. Reading and conversation may acquaint us with many truths, and with many arguments to support them; but it is our own study and reasoning that must determine whether these propositions are true, and whether these arguments are just and solid.

It is confessed there are a thousand things which our eyes have not seen, and which would never come within the reach of our personal and immediate knowledge and observation, . . . these must be known by consulting other persons; and that is done either in their writings or in their discourses. But after all, let this be a fixed point with us, that it is our own reflection and judgment must determine how far we should receive that which books or men inform us of, and how far they are worthy of our assent and credit.

(b) It is meditation . . . that **transfers and conveys the notions and sentiments of others to ourselves,** so as to make them properly our own. It is our own judgment upon them, as well as our memory of them, that makes them become our own property. It does as it were concoct our intellectual food, and turns it into a part of ourselves: . . .

(c) By study and meditation **we improve the hints that we have acquired by observation, conversation, *lecture*, and reading**: we take more time in thinking, and by the labour of the mind we penetrate deeper into the themes of knowledge, and carry our thoughts sometimes much farther on many subjects, than we ever met with, either in the books of the dead or discourses of the living. It is our own reasoning that draws out one truth from another, and forms a whole scheme or science from a few hints which we borrowed elsewhere.

- *Balance* -

By a survey of these things we may justly conclude, that he who spends all his time in hearing lectures, or poring upon books, without observation, meditation, or ... *conversation*, will have but a mere historical knowledge of learning, and be able only to tell what others have known or said on the subject: he that lets all his time flow away in conversation, without due observation, reading, or study, will gain but a slight and superficial knowledge, which will be in danger of vanishing with the voice of the speaker: and he that confines himself merely to his closet, and his own narrow observation of things, and is taught only by his own solitary thoughts, without instruction by lectures, reading, or free conversation, will be in danger of a narrow spirit, a vain conceit of himself, and an unreasonable contempt of others; and after all, he will obtain but a very limited and imperfect view and knowledge of things, and he will seldom learn how to make that knowledge useful.

- *Conclusion* -

These five methods of improvement should be pursued jointly, and go hand in hand, where our circumstances are so happy as to find opportunity and conveniency to enjoy them all: though I must give my opinion that two of them, viz., reading and meditation, should employ much more of our time than public lectures, or conversation and discourse. As for observation, we may be always acquiring knowledge that way, whether we are alone or in company.

But it will be for our further improvement, if we go over all these five methods of obtaining knowledge more distinctly and more at large, and see what special advances in useful science we may draw from them all.

Chapter 3

RULES RELATING TO OBSERVATION

Though observation, in the strict sense of the word, and as it is distinguished from meditation . . ., is the first means of improvement, and in its strictest sense does not include in it any reasonings of the mind upon the things which we observe, or inferences drawn from them; yet the motions of the mind are so *exceedingly* swift, that it is hardly possible for a thinking man to gain experiences or observations without making some secret and short reflections upon them: and therefore, in giving a few directions concerning this method of improvement, I shall not so narrowly confine myself to the first mere impression of objects on the mind by observation; but include also some hints which relate to the first, most easy and obvious reflections or reasoning which arise from them.

- Rules -

(1) **Let the enlargement of your knowledge be one constant view and design in life**, since there is no time or place, no transactions, occurrences, or engagements in life, which exclude us from this method of improving the mind. When we are alone, even in darkness and silence, we may converse with our own hearts, observe the working of our own spirits, and reflect upon the inward motions of our own passions in some of the latest occurrences in life; we may acquaint ourselves with the powers and properties, the tendencies and inclinations both of body and spirit, and gain a more intimate knowledge of ourselves. When we are in company, we may discover something more of human nature, of human passions and follies, and of human affairs, vices, and virtues, by conversing with mankind, and observing their conduct. . . .

When we are in the house or the city, wheresoever we turn our eyes, we see the works of men; ... The skies and the ground above and beneath us, and the animal and vegetable world round about us, may entertain our observation with ten thousand varieties.

Endeavour therefore to derive some instruction or improvement of the mind from every thing which you see or hear, from every thing which occurs in human life, from every thing within you or without you.

Fetch down some knowledge from the clouds, the stars, the sun, the moon, and the revolutions of all the planets. Dig and draw up some valuable meditations from the depths of the earth, and search them through the vast oceans of water. Extract some intellectual improvements from the minerals and metals; from the wonders of nature among the vegetables and herbs, trees and flowers. Learn some lessons from the birds and the beasts, and the meanest insect. ...

From the day and the night, the hours and the flying minutes, learn a wise improvement of time, and be watchful to seize every opportunity to increase in knowledge.

From the vicissitudes and revolutions of nations and families, and from the various occurrences of the world, learn the instability of mortal affairs, the uncertainty of life, the certainty of death. From a coffin and a funeral, learn to meditate upon your own departure.

From the vices and follies of others, observe what is hateful in them; consider how such a practice looks in another person, and remember that it looks as ill or worse in yourself. From the virtue of others learn something worthy of your imitation. ...

Thus from every appearance in nature, and from every occurrence of life, you may derive natural, moral, and religious observations, to entertain your minds, as well as rules of conduct in the affairs relating to ... life ...

(2) In order to furnish the mind with a rich variety of ideas, **the laudable curiosity of young people should be indulged and gratified, rather than discouraged**. It is a very hopeful sign in young persons to see them curious in observing, and inquisitive in searching into the greatest part of things that occur; nor should such an inquiring temper be frowned into silence, nor be rigorously

restrained, but should rather be satisfied by proper answers given to all those queries.

For this reason also, where time and fortune allow it, young people should be led into company at proper seasons, should be carried abroad to see the fields, and the woods, and the rivers, the buildings, towns, and cities distant from their own dwelling; they should be entertained with the sight of strange birds, beasts, fishes, insects, vegetables, and productions both of nature and art of every kind, whether they are the products of their own or foreign nations: and in due time . . . they may travel under a wise inspector or tutor to different parts of the world for the same end, that they may bring home treasures of useful knowledge.

(3) Among all these observations **write down what is most remarkable and uncommon**: reserve these remarks in store for proper occasions, and at proper seasons take a review of them. Such a practice will give you a habit of useful thinking; this will secure the workings of your soul from running to waste; and by this means even your looser moments will turn to happy account . . .

And whatever useful observations have been made, let them be at least some part of the subject of your conversation among your friends at next meeting.

Let the circumstances or situations in life be what or where they will, a man should never neglect this improvement which may be derived from observation. Let him travel into the East or West Indies, and fulfil the duties of the military or the mercantile life there; let him rove *over* . . . the earth or the seas, for his own humour as a traveller, or pursue his diversions in what part of the world he pleases . . .: let prosperous or adverse fortune call him to the most distant parts of the globe; still let him carry on his knowledge and the improvement of his soul by wise observations. In due time, by this means, he may render himself some way useful to the societies of mankind. . . .

(4) Let us **keep our minds as free as possible from passions and prejudices**; for these will give a wrong turn to our observations both on persons and things. The eyes of a man in the jaundice make yellow observations on every thing; and the soul tinctured with any passion or prejudice, diffuses a false colour over the real appear-

ances of things, and disguises many of the common occurrences of life: it never beholds things in a true light, nor suffers them to appear as they are. Whensoever, therefore, you would make proper observations, let self, with all its influences, stand aside as far as possible: abstract your own interest and your own concern from them, and bid all friendships and enmities stand aloof and keep out of the way, in the observations that you make relating to persons and things.

If this rule were well obeyed, we should be much better guarded against those common pieces of misconduct in the observations of men, viz., the false judgments of pride and envy. How ready is envy to mingle with the notices which we take of other persons? How often is mankind prone to put an ill sense upon the actions of their neighbours, to take a survey of them in an evil position, and in an unhappy light? And by this means we form a worse opinion of our neighbours than they deserve; while at the same time pride and self-flattery tempt us to make unjust observations on ourselves in our own favour. In all the favourable judgments we pass concerning ourselves, we should allow a little abatement on this account.

(5) In making your observations on persons, ... *beware* **of indulging that busy curiosity which is ever inquiring into private and domestic affairs**, with an endless itch of learning the secret history of families. It is but seldom that such a prying curiosity attains any valuable ends; it often begets suspicions, jealousies and disturbances in households, and it is a frequent temptation to persons to defame their neighbours: some persons cannot help telling what they know: a busy-body is most liable to become a tattler upon every occasion.

(6) **Let your observation**, even of persons and their conduct, **be chiefly designed** in order **to lead you to a better acquaintance with things**, particularly with human nature; and to inform you what to imitate and what to avoid, rather than to furnish out matter for the evil passions of the mind, or the impertinences of discourse and reproaches of the tongue.

(7) Though it may be proper sometimes to make your observations concerning persons as well as things the subject of your discourse in learned or useful conversations, yet what **remarks you make on particular persons, especially to their disadvantage, should for the**

most part lie hid in your own breast, till some just and apparent occasion ... leads you to speak to them.

If the character or conduct which you observe be greatly culpable, it should so much the less be published. You may treasure up such remarks of the follies, indecencies, or vices of your neighbours, as may be a constant guard against your practice of the same, without exposing the reputation of your neighbour on that account. It is a good old rule that our conversation should rather be laid out on things than on persons; and this rule should generally be observed, unless names be concealed, wheresoever the faults or follies of mankind are our present theme. ...

(8) **Be not too hasty to erect general theories from a few particular observations, appearances, or experiments.** This is what the logicians call a false induction. When general observations are drawn from so many particulars as to become certain and indubitable, these are jewels of knowledge, ...: but they are therefore to be made with the greater care and caution, lest errors become large and diffusive, if we should mistake in these general notions.

A hasty determination of some universal principles, without a due survey of all the particular cases which may be included in them, is the way to lay a trap for our own understandings in their pursuit of any subject, and we shall often be taken captives into mistake and falsehood. ... *A* youth observed that on three Christmas days together ... there fell a good quantity of snow, and now hath writ it down in his almanack, as a part of his wise remarks on the weather, that it will always snow at Christmas. ... *Another lad* took notice ten times that there was a sharp frost when the wind was in the north-east; therefore in the middle of last July he almost expected it should freeze, because the weathercocks shewed him a north-east wind; and he was still more disappointed when he found it a very sultry season. It is the same hasty judgment that hath thrown scandal on a whole nation for the sake of some culpable characters belonging to several particular natives of that country; ...

Chapter 4

BOOKS AND READING

In this chapter, Dr. Watts emphasizes that judiciously selecting and reading books, magazines, and articles with the serious intent of absorbing the knowledge that they contain is not a leisurely activity. It requires that we develop attitudes and strategies that will sharpen our comprehension and lead us to examine the validity and rationality of the material.

- Selecting Books -

The world is full of books; but there are multitudes which are so ill written, they were never worth any man's reading: and there are thousands more which may be good in their kind, yet are worth nothing when the month or year, or occasion is past for which they were written. Others may be valuable in themselves for some special purpose, or in some peculiar science; but are not fit to be perused by any but those who are engaged in that particular science or business. To what use is it for a divine or physician, or a tradesman, to read over the huge volumes of reports of judged cases in the law ... or for a lawyer to learn Hebrew, and read the Rabbins? **It is of vast advantage** for improvement of knowledge, and saving time, for a young man **to have the most proper books for** his **reading recommended by a judicious friend.**

- Books of Importance -

(1) **Books of importance of any kind,** and especially complete treatises on any subject, **should be first read in a more general and cursory manner,** to learn a little what the treatise promises, and what you may expect from the writer's manner and skill. And for this end I would advise always, that the preface be read, and a survey taken of the table of contents, if there be one, before the first survey of

the book. By this means you will not only be better fitted to give the book the first reading, but you will be much assisted in your second perusal of it, which should be done with greater attention and deliberation, and you will learn with more ease and readiness what the author pretends to teach. In your reading, mark what is new or unknown to you before, and review those chapters, pages, or paragraphs. Unless a reader has an uncommon and most retentive memory, I may venture to affirm, that there is scarce any book or chapter worth reading once, that is not worthy of a second perusal. At least to take a careful review of all the lines or paragraphs which you marked, and make a recollection of the sections which you thought truly valuable.

There is another reason also why I would choose to take a superficial and cursory survey of a book, before I sit down to read it, and dwell upon it with studious attention; and that is, there may be several difficulties in it which we cannot easily understand and conquer at the first reading, for want of a fuller comprehension of the author's whole scheme. And therefore in such treatises, we should not stay till we master every difficulty at the first perusal; for perhaps many of these would appear to be solved when we have proceeded further in that book, or would vanish of themselves upon a second reading.

What we cannot reach and penetrate at first may be noted down as a matter ... for further consideration and inquiry, if the pages that follow do not happen to strike a complete light on those which went before.

(2) **If three or four persons agree to read the same book**, and each bring his own remarks upon it, at some set hours appointed for conversation, and they communicate mutually their sentiments on the subject, and debate about it in a friendly manner, this practice **will render the reading** *of* any author more abundantly **beneficial to every one of them**.

(3) If **several persons engaged in the same study** take into their hands distinct treatises on one subject, and appoint a season of communication once a week, they may inform each other in a brief manner concerning the sense, sentiments, and method of those several authors, and thereby **promote each other's improvement**, either by recommending the perusal of the same book to their companions,

or perhaps by satisfying their inquiries concerning it by conversation, without every one's perusing it.

(4) Remember that your business in reading or in conversation, especially on subjects of natural, moral, or divine science, is not merely to know the opinion of the author or speaker, for this is but the mere knowledge of history; but **your chief business is to consider whether their opinions are right or no, and to improve your own solid knowledge** on that subject by meditation on the themes of their writing or discourse. Deal freely with every author you read, and yield up your assent only to evidence and just reasoning on the subject. . . .

But in the composures of men, remember you are a man as well as they; and it is not their reason but your own that is given to guide you when you arrive at years of discretion, of manly age and judgment.

(5) Let this therefore be your practice, especially after you have gone through one course of any science in your academical studies; **if a writer** on that subject maintains the same sentiments as you do, yet if he **does not explain his ideas or prove the positions well, mark the faults or defects, and endeavour to do it better**, either in the margin of your book, or rather in some papers of your own, or at least let it be done in your private meditations. As for instance: where the author is obscure, enlighten him: where he is imperfect, supply his deficiencies: where he is too brief and concise, amplify a little, and set his notions in a fairer view: where he is redundant, mark those paragraphs to be retrenched: when he trifles and grows impertinent, abandon those passages or pages: where he argues, observe whether his reasons be conclusive: if the conclusion be true, and yet the argument weak, endeavour to confirm it by better proofs: where he derives or infers any propositions darkly or doubtfully, make the justice of the inference appear, and make further inferences or corollaries, if such occur to your mind: where you suppose he is in a mistake, propose your objections and correct his sentiments: what he writes so well as to approve itself of your judgment, both as just and useful, treasure it up in your memory, and count it a part of your intellectual gains.

Note, many of these same directions which I have now given, may be practised with regard to conversation, as well as reading, in order to render it useful in the most extensive and lasting manner.

(6) ... **If the method of a book be irregular, reduce it into form by a little analysis of your own**, or by hints in the margin: if those things are heaped together, which should be separated, you may wisely distinguish and divide them: if several things relating to the same subject are scattered up and down separately through the treatise, you may bring them all to one view by references; or if the matter of a book be really valuable and deserving, you may throw it into a better method, reduce it to a more logical scheme, or abridge it into a lesser form: all these practices will have a tendency both to advance your skill in logic and method, to improve your judgment in general, and to give you a fuller survey of that subject in particular. When you have finished the treatise with all your observations upon it, recollect and determine what real improvements you have made by reading that author.

(7) **If a book has no index to it, or good table of contents**, it is very useful to **make one** as you are reading it: not with that exactness as to include the sense of every page and paragraph, which should be done if you designed to print it; but it is sufficient in your index to take notice only of those parts of the book which are new to you, or which you think well written, and well worthy of your remembrance or review.

Shall I be so free as to assure my younger friends, from my own experience, that these methods of reading will cost some pains in the first years of your study, and especially in the first authors which you peruse in any science, or on any particular subject: but the profit will richly compensate the pains. And in the following years of life, after you have read a few valuable books on any special subject in this manner, it will be very easy to read others of the same kind, because you will not usually find very much new matter in them which you have not already examined.

If the writer be remarkable for any peculiar excellencies or defects in his style or manner of writing, make just observations upon this also; and whatsoever ornaments you find there, or whatsoever blemishes occur in the language or manner of the writer, you may make just remarks upon them. And remember that one book read over in this manner, with all this laborious meditation, will tend more to enrich your understanding, than the skimming over the surface of twenty authors.

(8) By perusing books in the manner I have described, you will **make all your reading subservient not only to the enlargement of your treasures of knowledge, but also to the improvement of your reasoning powers.**

There are many who read with constancy and diligence, and yet make no advances in true knowledge by it. They are delighted with the notions which they read or hear, as they would be with stories that are told; but they do not weigh them in their minds as in a just balance, in order to determine their truth or falsehood; they make no observations upon them, or inferences from them. . . .

Or if they review them sufficiently to fix them in their remembrance, it is merely with a design to tell the tale over again, and shew what men of learning they are. Thus they dream out their days in a course of reading, without real advantage. As a man may be eating all day, and for want of digestion is never nourished; so these endless readers may cram themselves in vain with intellectual food, and without real improvement of their minds, for want of digesting it by proper reflections.

(9) **Be diligent** therefore in observing these directions. Enter **into the sense and arguments of the authors** you read; examine all their proofs, and then judge of the truth or falsehood of their opinions; and thereby you shall not only gain a rich increase of your understanding, by those truths which the author teaches, when you see them well supported, but you shall acquire also by degrees a habit of judging justly, and of reasoning well, in imitation of the good writer whose works you peruse.

This is laborious indeed, and the mind is backward to undergo the fatigue of weighing every argument, and tracing every thing to its original. It is much less labour to take all things upon trust: believing is much easier than arguing. . . .

I confess those whose reading is designed only to fit them for much talk, and little knowledge, may content themselves to run over their authors in such a sudden and trifling way; they may devour libraries in this manner, yet be poor reasoners at last; and have no solid wisdom or true learning. The traveler who walks on fair and softly in a course that points right, and examines every turning before he ventures upon it, will come sooner and safer to his journey's end, than he who runs through every lane he meets, though he gallops full speed all the day. The man of much reading, and a large retentive memory, but without meditation, may become in the sense of the world a knowing man; and if he converse much with the ancients, he may attain the fame of learning too; but he spends his days afar off from wisdom and true judgment, and possesses very little of the substantial riches of the mind.

(10) **Never apply yourselves to read any ... author with a determination beforehand either for or against him**, or with a settled resolution to believe, or disbelieve, to confirm or to oppose, whatsoever he saith; but always read with a design to lay your mind open to truth, and to embrace it wheresoever you find it, as well as to reject every falsehood, though it appear under ever so fair a disguise. How unhappy are those men who seldom take an author into their hands but they have determined before they begin, whether they will like or dislike him! They have got some notion of his name, his character, his party, or his principles, by general conversation, or perhaps by some slight view of a few pages; and having all their own opinions adjusted beforehand, they read all that he writes with a prepossession either for or against him. Unhappy *are* those who hunt and purvey for a party, and scrape together out of every author, all those things, and those only, which favour their own tenets, while they despise and neglect all the rest!

Yet take this caution. I would not be understood here, as though I persuaded a person to live without any settled principles at all, by which to judge of men, and books, and things: or that I would keep a man always doubting about his foundations. The chief things that I design in this advice, are these three:

(a) That after our most necessary and important principles of science, prudence, and religion are settled upon good grounds, with regard to our present conduct and our future hopes, we should read with a just freedom of thought, all those books which treat of such subjects as may admit of doubt and reasonable dispute. **Nor should any of our opinions be so**

resolved upon, especially in younger years, as never to hear or to bear an opposition to them.

(b) **When we peruse those authors who defend our own settled sentiments, we should not take all their arguments for just and solid**; but we should make a wise distinction between the corn and the chaff, between solid reasoning and the mere superficial colours of it; nor should we readily swallow down all their lesser opinions because we agree with them in the greater.

(c) That **when we read those authors which oppose our most certain and established principles, we should be ready to receive any informations from them in other points,** and not abandon at once every thing they say, though we are well fixed in our opposition to their main point of arguing.

> Seize upon truth where'er 'tis found,
> Amongst your friends, amongst your foes,
> On Christian or on Heathen ground;
> The flower's divine where'er it grows,
> Neglect the prickles and assume the rose.

(11) What I have said hitherto on this subject, relating to books and reading, must be chiefly understood of that sort of books, and those hours of our reading and study, whereby we design to improve the intellectual powers of the mind with natural, *and* moral ... knowledge. As for those treatises which are written to direct or to enforce and persuade our practice, there is one thing further necessary; and that is, that **when our consciences are convinced that these rules of prudence or duty belong to us, and require our conformity to them, we should then call ourselves to account,** and inquire seriously whether we have put them in practice or no, we should dwell upon the arguments, and impress the motives and methods of persuasion upon our own hearts, till we feel the force and power of them inclining us to the practice of the things which are there recommended. ...

- *Books of Diversion and Amusement* -

There is yet another sort of books, of which it is proper I should say something, while I am treating on this subject; and these are, **history, poesy, travels,** *fiction* ... ; among which we may reckon also little common pamphlets, newspapers, or such like: for many of these I confess once reading may be sufficient, where there is a tolerable good memory.

(1) Or when several persons are in company, and one reads to the rest such sort of writings, once hearing may be sufficient, provided that every one be so attentive, and so free, as to make their occasional remarks on such lines or sentences, ... as in their opinion deserve it. Now **all those paragraphs or sentiments deserve a remark, which are new and uncommon, are noble and excellent** for the matter of them, are **strong and convincing** for the argument contained in them, are **beautiful and elegant** for the language or the manner, **or any way worthy** of a second rehearsal; and at the request of any of the company let those paragraphs be read over again.

(2) Such parts also of these **writings as may happen to be remarkably stupid or silly, false or mistaken, should become subjects of an occasional criticism,** made by some of the company; and this may give occasion to the repetition of them for the confirmation of the censure, for amusement or diversion.

(3) Still let it be remembered, that where the historical narration is of considerable moment, **where the poesy, oratory, etc. shine** with some degrees of perfection and glory, **a single reading is *not* sufficient** to satisfy a mind that has a true taste of this sort of writings; nor can we make the fullest and best improvement of them without proper reviews, and that in our retirement as well as in company. Who is there that has any ... *appreciation* for polite writings that would be sufficiently satisfied with hearing the beautiful pages of Steele or Addison, the admirable descriptions of Virgil or Milton, or some of the finest poems of Pope, Young, or Dryden, once read over to them, and then lay them by for ever?

Among these writings of the latter kind we may justly reckon short miscellaneous essays on all manner of subjects; such as the Occasional Papers, the Tatlers, the Spectators, and some other books that have been compiled out of the weekly or daily products of the press, wherein are contained a great number of bright thoughts, ingenious remarks, and admirable observations, which have had a considerable share in furnishing the present age with knowledge and politeness.

I wish every paper among these writings could have been recommended both as innocent and useful. I wish every unseemly idea and wanton expression had been banished from amongst them, and every trifling page had been excluded from the company of the rest when they had been bound up in volumes: but it is not to be expected, in so imperfect a state, that every page or piece of such mixed public papers should be entirely blameless and laudable. Yet in the main it must be confessed, there is so much virtue, prudence, ingenuity, and goodness in them, . . . so many valuable remarks for our conduct in life, that they are not improper to lie in parlours, or summer-houses, or places of usual residence, to entertain our thoughts in any moments of leisure, or vacant hours that occur. There is such a discovery of the follies, iniquities, and fashionable vices of mankind contained in them, that we may learn much of the humours and madnesses of the age and the public world, in our own solitary retirement, . . .

- Books that Sharpen Our Literary Comprehension -

(1) Among other books which are proper and requisite, in order to improve our knowledge in general, or our acquaintance with any particular science, it is necessary that we should be furnished with **vocabularies and dictionaries** of several sorts, viz. of common words, idioms, and phrases, in order to explain their sense; of technical words or the terms of art, to shew their use in arts and sciences; of names of men, countries, towns, rivers, etc. which are called historical and geographical dictionaries, etc. These **are to be consulted** and used upon every occasion; **and never let an unknown word pass in your reading without seeking for its sense and meaning** in some of these writers.

If such books are not at hand, you must supply the want of them as well as you can, by consulting such as can inform you: and it is useful to note down the matters of doubt and inquiry in some pocket-book, and take the first opportunity to get them resolved, either by persons or books, when we meet with them.

- Scholar vs. Mere Collector -

(1) **Be not satisfied with a mere knowledge of the best authors that treat of any subject,** instead of acquainting yourselves thoroughly with the subject itself. There is many a young student that is fond of

enlarging his knowledge of books, and he contents himself with the notice he has of their title-page, which is the attainment of a bookseller rather than a scholar. Such persons are under a great temptation to practise these two follies:

(a) To heap up a great number of books at a greater expense than most of them can bear, and to **furnish their libraries infinitely better than their understanding**. . . .

(b) When they have gotten such rich treasures of knowledge upon their shelves, they imagine themselves men of learning, and take a pride in talking of the names of famous authors, and the subjects of which they treat, without any real improvement of their own minds in true science or wisdom. **At best their learning reaches no further than the indexes and table of contents**, while they know not how to judge or reason concerning the matters contained in those authors.

And indeed how many volumes of learning soever a man possesses, he is still deplorably poor in his understanding, till he has made those several parts of learning his own property by reading and reasoning, by judging for himself, and remembering what he has read.

Chapter 5

JUDGMENT OF BOOKS

In this chapter Dr. Watts recommends that we learn to judge books objectively on the merits of their content, thoroughness, organization, and logic, regardless of our own biases and preferences concerning the subjects and authors.

(1) **If we would form a judgment of a book which we have not seen before**, the first thing that offers, is **the title-page**, and we may sometimes guess a little at the import and design of a book thereby; though it must be confessed that titles are often deceitful, and promise more than the book performs. **The author's name**, if it be known in the world, may help us to conjecture at the performance a little more, and lead us to guess in what manner it is done. A perusal of **the preface** or introduction (which I before recommended) **may** further **assist our judgment**; and if there be an index of the contents, it will give us still some advancing light.

If we have not leisure or inclination to read over the book itself regularly, then by the titles of chapters we may be directed to peruse several particular chapters or sections, and observe whether there be any thing valuable or important in them. We shall find hereby whether the author explains his ideas clearly, whether he reasons strongly, whether he methodizes well, whether his thought and sense be manly and his manner polite; or on the other hand, whether he be obscure, weak, trifling, and confused; or finally, whether the matter may not be solid and substantial, though the style and manner be rude and disagreeable.

(2) By having run through several chapters and sections in this manner, we may generally **judge whether the treatise be worth a complete**

perusal or no. But if by such an occasional survey of some chapters our expectation be utterly discouraged, we may well lay aside that book; for there is great probability he can be but an indifferent writer on that subject, ... The piece can hardly be valuable if in seven or eight chapters which we peruse there be but little truth, evidence, force of reasoning, beauty, and ingenuity of thought, etc. mingled with much error, ignorance, impertinence, dulness, mean and common thoughts, inaccuracy, sophistry, railing, etc. Life is too short, and time is too precious, to read every new book quite over in order to find that is not worth the reading.

(3) There are some **general mistakes** which persons are frequently guilty of in passing a judgment on the books which they read.

    (a) One is this; when a treatise is written but tolerable well, **we are ready to pass a favourable judgment** of it, and sometimes to exalt its character far beyond its merit, **if it agree with our own principles**, and support the opinions of our party. On the other hand, if the author be of different sentiments, and espouse contrary principles, we can find neither wit nor reason, good sense, nor good language in it; whereas, alas! if our opinions of things were certain and infallible truth, yet a silly author may draw his pen in the defence of them, and he may attack even gross errors with feeble and ridiculous arguments. Truth in this world is not always attended and supported by the wisest and safest methods; and error, though it can never be maintained by just reasoning, yet may be artfully covered and defended. An ingenious writer may put excellent colours upon his own mistakes. ... Books are never to be judged of merely by their subject, or the opinion they represent, but by the justness of their sentiment, the beauty of their manner, the force of their expression, or the strength of reason, and the weight of just and proper argument which appears in them.

    (b) Another mistake which some persons fall into is this: when they read a treatise on a subject with which they have but little acquaintance, they find almost every thing new and strange to them: their understandings are greatly entertained and improved by the occurrence of many things which were unknown to them before; **they admire the treatise**, and commend the author at once; **whereas if they had but attained a good degree**

of skill in that science, perhaps they would find that the author had written very poorly, that neither his sense nor his method was just and proper, and that he had nothing in him but what was very common or trivial in his discourses on that subject.

. . .

(c) But there is a danger of mistake in our judgment of books, on the other hand also: for **when we have made ourselves masters of any particular theme of knowledge,** and surveyed it long on all sides, there is perhaps scarce any writer on that subject who much entertains and pleases us afterwards, because we find little or nothing new in him; and yet, in a true judgment, perhaps his sentiments are most proper and just, his explication clear, and his reasoning strong, and all the parts of the discourse are well connected and set in a happy light; but **we knew most of those things before, and therefore they strike us not and we are in danger of discommending them.**

Thus the learned and the unlearned have their several distinct dangers and prejudices ready to attend them in their judgment of the writings of men. . . .

(4) Yet I cannot forbear to point out . . . **more of these follies,** that I may attempt something towards the correction of them, or at least to guard others against them.

    (a) **There are some persons** of a forward and lively temper, and who are fond to intermeddle with all appearances of knowledge, **will give their judgment on a book as soon as the title of it is mentioned,** *though they have neither studied nor understood it,* for they would not willingly seem ignorant of any thing that others know. And especially if they happen to have any superior character or possessions of this world, they fancy they have a right to talk freely upon every thing that stirs or appears, though they have no other pretence to this freedom. . . . But this is the way of the world; . . . *For example,* those who have nothing to do with religion, will arraign the best treatise on divine subjects, though they do not understand the very language of the scripture, nor the common terms or phrases used in Christianity.

(b) I might here name **another sort of judges**, who will set themselves up to decide in favour of an author, or will pronounce him a mere blunderer, according to the company they have kept, and the judgment they have heard passed upon a book by others of their own stamp or size, though they have no knowledge or taste of the subject themselves. These, with a fluent and voluble tongue, **become mere echoes of the praises or censures of other men.** . . .

(5) There is yet another mischievous principle, which prevails among some persons in passing a judgment on the writings of others, and that is, when from the secret stimulations of vanity, pride, or envy, they despise a valuable book, and throw contempt upon it by wholesale: and if you ask them the reason of their severe censure, they will tell you, perhaps, they have found a mistake or two in it, or there are a few sentiments or expressions not suited to their tooth and humour. . . . **It is a paltry humour that inclines a man to rail at any human performance because it is not absolutely perfect.** Horace would give us a better example *as translated by Roscommon*:

Be not too rigidly censorious:
A string may jar in the best master's hand,
And the most skilful archer miss his aim:
So in a poem elegantly writ,
I will not quarrel with a small mistake,
Such as our nature's frailty may excuse.

This noble translator of Horace, whom I here cite, has a very honourable opinion of Homer in the main; yet he allows him to be justly censured for some grosser spots and blemishes in him:

For who without aversion ever look'd
On holy garbage, though by Homer cook'd;
Whose railing heroes, and whose wounded gods,
Make some suspect he snores as well as nods.

Such wise and just distinctions ought to be made when we pass a judgment on mortal things; but Envy condemns by wholesale. Envy is a cursed plant; some fibres of it are rooted almost in every man's nature, and it works in a sly and imperceptible manner, and that even in some persons who in the main are men of wisdom and piety. They know not how to bear the praises that are given to an ingenious author, especially if he be living, and of their profession; and therefore they will, if possible, find some blemish in his writings, that they may nibble and bark at it. They will endeavour to diminish the honour of the best treatise that has been written on any subject, and to render it useless by their censures, rather than suffer their envy to lie asleep, and the little mistakes of that author to pass unexposed. Perhaps they will commend the work in general with a pretended air of candour; but pass so many sly and invidious remarks upon it afterwards, as shall effectually destroy all their cold and formal praises.

When a person feels any thing of this invidious humour working in him, he may by the following consideration attempt the correction of it. Let him think with himself how many are the beauties of such an author whom he censures, in comparison of his blemishes, and remember that it is a much more honourable and good-natured thing to find out peculiar beauties than faults; true and undisguised candour is a much more amiable and divine talent than accusation. Let him reflect again, what an easy matter it is to find a mistake in all ... authors, who are necessarily fallible and imperfect. ...

But where an author has many beauties consistent with virtue, piety, and truth, let not little critics exalt themselves, and shower down their ill-nature upon him, without bounds or measure, but rather stretch their own powers of soul till they write a treatise superior to that which they condemn. This is the noblest and surest manner of suppressing what they censure. ...

(6) **Another**, and that a **very frequent fault**, in passing a judgment upon books, **is this, that persons spread the same praises or the same reproaches over a whole treatise, and all the chapters in it, which are due only to some of them.** They judge as it were by wholesale, without making a due distinction between the several parts or sections of the performance; and this is ready to lead those who hear them talk into a dangerous mistake. ...

Milton is a noble genius, and the world agrees to confess it; his poem of Paradise Lost is a glorious performance, and rivals the most famous pieces of antiquity; but that reader must be deeply prejudiced in favour of the poet, who can imagine him equal to himself through all that work. Neither the sublime sentiments, ... nor force or beauty of expression, are equally maintained, even in all those parts which require grandeur or beauty, force or harmony. ...

(7) **When you hear any person pretending to give his judgment of a book, consider** with yourself **whether he be a capable judge,** or whether he may not lie under some unhappy bias or prejudice, for or against it, or whether he has made a sufficient inquiry to form his justest sentiments upon it. ...

If you find that he is either an unfit judge because of his ignorance or because of his prejudices, his judgment of that book should go for nothing.

Chapter 6

LIVING INSTRUCTIONS AND LECTURES; TEACHERS AND LEARNERS

In this chapter, Dr. Watts emphasizes the effectiveness of learning from lectures when the lecturer is possessed with not only the necessary expertise but also with the abilities to communicate, motivate, and set an admirable example.

There are a few persons of so penetrating a genius, and so just a judgment, as to be capable of learning the arts and sciences without the **assistance of teachers**. There is scarce any science so safely and so speedily learned, even by the noblest genius ..., without a tutor. His assistance **is absolutely necessary for most persons**, and it is very useful for all beginners. Books are a sort of dumb teachers; they point out the way to learning; but if we labour under any doubt or mistake, they cannot answer sudden questions, or explain present doubts and difficulties: this is properly the work of a living instructor.

- Selection of Instructors -

(1) There are very few tutors who are sufficiently furnished with such universal learning, as to sustain all the parts and provinces of instruction. The sciences are numerous, and many of them lie far wide of each other; and **it is best to enjoy the instructions of two or three tutors at least**, in order to run through the whole encyclopaedia, or circle of sciences, where it may be obtained; then we may expect that each will teach the few parts of learning which are committed to his care in greater perfection. ...

(2) It is not sufficient that **instructors** be competently skilful in those sciences which they profess and teach; but they **should have skill**

also **in the art or method of teaching, and patience in the practice of it.**

It is a great unhappiness indeed, when persons by a spirit of party, or faction, or interest, or by purchase, are set up for tutors, who have neither due knowledge of science, nor skill in the way of communication. And alas! there are others who, with all their ignorance and insufficiency, have self-admiration and effrontery enough to set up themselves; and the poor pupils fare accordingly, and grow lean in their understandings.

And let it be observed also, there are some very learned men who know much themselves, but have not the talent of communicating their own knowledge; or else they are lazy, and will take no pains at it. Either they have an obscure and perplexed way of talking, or they shew their learning uselessly, and make a long periphrasis on every word of the book they explain, or they cannot condescend to young beginners, or they run presently into the elevated parts of the science, because it gives themselves greater pleasure, or they are soon angry and impatient, and cannot bear with a few impertinent questions of a young inquisitive and sprightly genius; or else they skim over a science in a very slight and superficial survey, and never lead their disciples into the depths of it.

(3) **A good tutor** should have characters and qualifications very different from all these. He is such a one as both can and **will apply himself with diligence and concern**, and indefatigable patience, to effect what he undertakes; to teach his disciples, and see that they learn; to adapt his way and method, as near as may be, to the various dispositions, as well as to the capacities of those whom he instructs, and to inquire often into their progress and improvement.

(4) ... *The tutor* **should take particular care** of his own temper and conduct, **that there be nothing in him** or about him **which may be of ill example**; nothing that may savour of a haughty temper, or a mean and sordid spirit; nothing that may expose him to the aversion or to the contempt of his scholars, or create a prejudice in their minds against him and his instructions: but, if possible, he should have so much of a natural candour and sweetness mixed with all the improvements of learning, as might convey knowledge into the minds of his disciples with a sort of gentle insinuation and

sovereign delight, and may tempt them into the highest improvements of their reason by a resistless and insensible force. But I shall have occasion to say more on this subject, when I come to speak more directly of the methods of the communication of knowledge.

- *Rules for the Learner* -

(1) **The learner should attend with constancy and care on all the instructions of his tutor**; and if he happens to be at any time unavoidably hindered, he must endeavour to retrieve the loss by double industry for time to come. He should always recollect and review his lectures, read over some other author or authors upon the same subject, confer upon it with his instructor, or with his associates, and write down the clearest result of his present thoughts, reasonings, and inquiries, which he may have recourse to hereafter, either to re-examine them and to apply them to proper use, or to improve them farther to his own advantage.

(2) **A student should never satisfy himself with bare attendance** on the lectures of his tutor, unless he clearly takes up his sense and meaning, and understands the things which he teaches. A young disciple should behave himself so well as to gain the affection and ear of his instructor, that upon every occasion he may, with the utmost freedom, ask questions, and talk over his own sentiments, his doubts and difficulties with him, and in a humble and modest manner desire the solution of them.

(3) **Let the learner endeavour to maintain an honourable opinion of his instructor**, and heedfully listen to his instructions, as one willing to be led by a more experienced guide; and though he is not bound to fall in with every sentiment of his tutor, yet he should so far comply with him as to resolve upon a just consideration of the matter, and try and examine it thoroughly with an honest heart, before he presume to determine against him: and then it should be done with great modesty, ...

(a) It is a frequent and growing folly in our age, that **pert young disciples soon fancy themselves wiser than those who teach them**: at the first view, or upon a very little thought, they can discern the insignificancy, weakness, and mistake of what their teacher asserts. The youth of our day, by an early petulancy, and pretended liberty of thinking for themselves, dare reject at

once, and that with a sort of scorn, all those sentiments and doctrines which their teachers have determined perhaps after long and repeated consideration, after years of mature study, careful observation, and much prudent experience.

(b) It is true, **teachers and masters are not infallible**, nor are they always in the right; and it must be acknowledged, it is a matter of some difficulty for younger minds to maintain a just and solemn veneration for the authority and advice of their parents and the instructions of their tutors, and yet at the same time to secure to themselves a just freedom in their own thoughts. We are sometimes too ready to imbibe all their sentiments without examination, if we reverence and love them; or, on the other hand, if we take all freedom to contest their opinions, we are sometimes tempted to cast off that love and reverence to their persons. ... Youth is ever in danger of these two extremes.

(4) But I think I may safely conclude thus: though the **authority of a teacher must not absolutely determine the judgment of his pupil**, yet young and raw and unexperienced learners should pay all proper deference that can be to the instructions of their parents and teachers, short of absolute submission to their dictates. Yet still we must maintain this, that they should never receive any opinion into their assent, whether it be conformable or contrary to the tutor's mind, without sufficient evidence of it first given to their own reasoning powers.

Chapter 7

RULES OF IMPROVEMENT BY CONVERSATION

In this chapter, Dr. Watts recommends several methods of improvement by conversation, such as conversing with those who are wiser than we and those who have different professions and interests. He discusses the advantages of establishing conversation groups. He stresses that keeping an atmosphere of cordiality and reasonableness in a dispute or query prevents the development of barriers to the free flow of information and the receptivity of the minds. Finally, he advises us to avoid those who practice "anything unbecoming to an open searcher of truth."

(1) If we would improve our minds by conversation, **it is a great happiness to be acquainted with persons wiser than ourselves.** It is a piece of useful advice therefore to get the favour of their conversation frequently, as far as circumstances will allow: and if they happen to be a little reserved, use all obliging methods to draw out of them what may increase your own knowledge.

(2) Whatsoever company you are in, **waste not the time in trifle and impertinence.** If you spend some hours amongst children, talk with them according to their capacity; mark the young buddings of infant reason; observe the different motions and distinct workings of the animal and the mind, as far as you can discern them; take notice by what degrees the little creature grows up for the use of his reasoning powers, and what early prejudices beset and endanger his understanding. By this means you will learn how to address yourself to children for their benefit, and perhaps you may derive some useful philosophemes or theorems for your own entertainment.

(3) If you happen to be in company with a merchant or a sailor, a farmer or a mechanic, a milkmaid or a spinster, **lead them into a discourse of the matters of their own peculiar province or profession**; for every one knows, or should know, their own business best. In this sense a common mechanic is wiser than the philosopher. By this means you may gain some improvement in knowledge from every one you meet.

(4) **Confine not yourself always to one sort of company,** or to persons of the same party or opinion, either in matters of learning, religion, or the civil life, **lest,** if you should happen to be nursed up or educated in *an* early mistake, **you should be confirmed and established in the same mistake, by conversing only with persons of the same sentiments.** A free and general conversation with men of very various countries, and of different parties, opinions, and practices, so far as it may be done safely, is of excellent use to un-deceive us in many wrong judgments which we may have framed, and to lead us into juster thoughts. It is said, when the King of Siam, near China, first conversed with some European merchants, who sought the favour of trading on his coast, he inquired of them some of the common appearances of summer and winter in their country; and when they told him of water growing so hard in their rivers, that men and horses and laden carriages passed over it, and that rain sometimes fell down as white and light as feathers, and sometimes almost as hard as stones, he would not believe a syllable they said; for ice, snow, and hail, were names and things utterly unknown to him and to his subjects, in that hot climate: he renounced all traffic with such shameful liars, and would not suffer them to trade with his people. See here the natural effects of gross ignorance. ...

(5) **In mixed company among acquaintance and strangers, endeavour to learn something from all.** Be swift to hear; but be cautious of your tongue, lest you betray your ignorance, and perhaps offend some of those who are present too. ... Acquaint yourself therefore sometimes with persons and parties which are far distant from your common life and customs: this is a way whereby you may form a wiser opinion of men and things. ...

(6) **Be not frighted nor provoked at opinions different from you own.** Some persons are so confident they are in the right, that they will

not come within the hearing of any notions but their own: they canton out to themselves a little province in the intellectual world, where they fancy the light shines; and all the rest is in darkness. They never venture into the ocean of knowledge, nor survey the riches of other minds, which are as solid and as useful, and perhaps are finer gold than what they ever possessed. Let not men imagine there is no certain truth but in the sciences which they study, and amongst that party in which they were born and educated.

(7) **Believe that it is possible to learn something from persons much below yourself.** We are all short-sighted creatures; our views are also narrow and limited; we often see but one side of a matter, and do not extend our sight far and wide enough to reach every thing that has a connexion with the thing we talk of: we see but in part, and know but in part; therefore it is no wonder we form not right conclusions; because we do not survey the whole of any subject or argument. Even the proudest admirer of his own parts might find it useful to consult with others, though of inferior capacity and penetration. We have a different prospect of the same thing ... according to the different position of our understandings towards it: a weaker man may sometimes light on notions which have escaped a wiser, and which the wiser man might make a happy use of, if he would condescend to take notice of them.

(8) **It is of considerable advantage, when we are pursuing any difficult point of knowledge, to have a society of ingenious correspondents at hand, to whom we may propose it**: for every man has something of a different genius and a various turn of mind, whereby the subject proposed will be shewn in all its lights, it will be represented in all its forms, and every side of it be turned to view, that a juster judgment may be framed.

(9) To make conversation more valuable and useful, whether it be in a designed or accidental visit, among persons of the same or of different sexes, after the necessary salutations are finished, and the stream of common talk begins to hesitate, or runs flat and low, **let some one person take a book which may be agreeable to the whole company, and by common consent let him read in it** ten lines, or a paragraph or two, or a few pages, till some word or sentence gives an occasion for any of the company to offer a thought or two relating to that subject: interruption of the reader should be no

blame; for conversation is the business: whether it be to confirm what the author says, or to improve it, to enlarge upon or to correct it, to object against it, or to ask any question that is akin to it; and let every one that please add their opinion and promote the conversation. When the discourse sinks again, or diverts to trifles, let him that reads pursue the page, and read on further paragraphs or pages, till some occasion is given by a word or sentence for a new discourse to be started, and that with the utmost ease and freedom. Such a method as this would prevent the hours of a visit from running all to waste; and by this means even among scholars, they would seldom find occasion for that too just and bitter reflection, "I have lost my time in the company of the learned." ...

(10) Observe this rule in general, **whensoever it lies in your power to lead the conversation, let it be directed to some profitable point of knowledge or practice**, so far as may be done with decency; and let not the discourse and the hours be suffered to run loose without aim or design: and when a subject is started, pass not hastily to another, before you have brought the present theme of discourse to some tolerable issue, or a joint consent to drop it.

(11) **Attend with sincere diligence**, while any one of the company is declaring his sense of the question proposed; hear the argument with patience, though it differ ever so much from your sentiments, for you yourself are very desirous to be heard with patience by others who differ from you. Let not your thoughts be active and busy all the while to find out something to contradict, and by what means to oppose the speaker, especially in matters which are not brought to an issue. This is a frequent and unhappy temper and practice. You should rather be intent and solicitous to take up the mind and meaning of the speaker, zealous to seize and approve all that is true in his discourse, nor yet should you want courage to oppose where it is necessary; but let your modesty and patience, and a friendly temper, be as conspicuous as your zeal.

(12) **When a man** speaks with much freedom and ease, and **gives his opinion in the plainest language of common sense, do not presently imagine you shall gain nothing by his company**. Sometimes you will find a person who, in his conversation or his writings, delivers his thoughts in so plain, so easy, so familiar, and perspicuous a manner, that you both understand and assent to every thing he

saith, as fast as you read or hear it: hereupon some hearers have been ready to conclude in haste, surely this man saith none but common things; I knew as much before, or, I would have said all this myself. This is a frequent mistake. . . .

(13) **If** any thing seem dark in the discourse of your companion, so that **you have not a clear idea of what is spoken, endeavour to obtain a clearer conception of it by a decent manner of inquiry.** Do not charge the speaker with obscurity, either in his sense or his words, but intreat his favour to relieve your own want of penetration, or to add an enlightening word or two, that you may take up his whole meaning.

(14) If difficulties arise in your mind, and constrain your dissent to the things spoken, **represent what objection some persons would be ready to make against the sentiments of the speaker, without telling him you oppose.** This manner of address carries something more modest and obliging in it, than to appear to raise objections of your own by way of contradiction to him that spoke.

(15) **When you are forced to differ** from him who delivers his sense on any point, yet agree as far as you can, and **represent how far you agree**; and if there be any room for it, explain the words of the speaker in such a sense to which you can in general assent, and so agree with him, or at least by a small addition or alteration of his sentiments shew your own sense of things. It is the practice and delight of a candid hearer, to make it appear how unwilling he is to differ from him that speaks. Let the speaker know that it is nothing but truth constrains you to oppose him; and let that difference be always expressed in a few, . . . civil, . . . chosen words, such as may give the least offense.

(16) . . . Be careful always to take Solomon's rule with you, and **let your correspondent fairly finish his speech before you reply;** 'for he that answereth a matter before he heareth it, it is folly and shame unto him.' Prov. XVIII. 13. . . .

(17) As you should carry about with you a constant and sincere sense of your own ignorance, so you should not be afraid nor ashamed to confess this ignorance, by taking all proper opportunities to ask and inquire for further information; whether it be the meaning of a word, the nature of a thing, the reason of a proposition,

the custom of a nation, etc. **never remain in ignorance for want of asking**.

Many a person had arrived at some considerable degree of knowledge, if he had not been full of self-conceit, and imagined that he had known enough already, or else was ashamed to let others know that he was unacquainted with it. ... he that fancies himself to know any particular subject well, or that will not venture to ask a question about it, such a one will not put himself into the way of improvement by inquiry and diligence. ... *He* is very likely to be an everlasting fool; and perhaps also it is a silly shame renders his folly incurable. ...

(18) **Be not too forward**, especially in the younger part of life, **to determine any question** in company **with an infallible and peremptory sentence**, nor speak with assuming airs, and with a decisive tone of voice. A young man, in the presence of his elders, should rather hear and attend, and weigh the arguments which are brought for the proof or refutation of any doubtful proposition: and when it is your turn to speak, propose your thoughts rather in the way of inquiry. By this means your mind will be kept in a fitter temper to receive truth, and you will be more ready to correct and improve your own sentiments, where you have not been too positive in affirming them. But if you have magisterially decided the point, you will find a secret unwillingness to retract, though you should feel an inward conviction that you were in the wrong.

(19) It is granted indeed, that a season may happen, when some bold pretender to science may assume haughty and positive airs, to assert and vindicate a gross and dangerous error, or to renounce and vilify some very important truth: and if he has a popular talent of talking, and there be no remonstrance made against him, the company may be tempted too easily to give their assent to the imprudence and infallibility of the presumer. They may imagine a proposition so much vilified can never be true; and that a doctrine which is so boldly censured and renounced can never be defended. Weak minds are too ready to persuade themselves, that a man would never talk with so much assurance unless he were certainly in the right, and could well maintain and prove what he said. By this means **truth itself is in danger of being betrayed or lost, if there be no opposition made to** such **a pretending talker**.

(a) Now in such a case, even **a wise and a modest man may** assume airs too, and **repel insolence with its own weapons.** There is a time, as Solomon ... teaches us, "when a fool should be answered according to his folly, lest he be wise in his own conceit," and lest others too easily yield up their faith and reason to his imperious dictates. Courage and positivity are never more necessary than on such an occasion. But it is good to join some argument with them of real and convincing force, and let it be strongly pronounced too.

(b) When such a resistance is made, you shall find some of those bold talkers will draw in their horns, when their fierce and feeble pushes against truth and reason are repelled with pushing and confidence. It is pity indeed that truth should ever need such sort of defences; but we know that **a triumphant assurance hath sometimes supported gross falsehoods, and a whole company have been captivated to error** by this means, **till some man with equal assurance has rescued them.** It is a pity that any momentous point of doctrine should happen to fall under such reproaches, and require such a mode of vindication: though if I happen to hear it I ought not to turn my back and to sneak off in silence, and leave the truth to lie baffled, bleeding, and slain. ...

(20) **Be not fond of disputing every thing pro and con,** nor indulge yourself to shew your talent of attacking and defending. A logic which teaches nothing else is *of* little worth. This temper and practice will lead you just so far out of the way of knowledge, and divert your honest inquiry after the truth which is debated or sought. In set disputes, every little straw is often laid hold on to support our own cause; every thing that can be drawn in any way to give colour to our argument is advanced, and that perhaps with vanity and ostentation. This puts the mind out of a proper posture to seek and receive the truth.

(21) **Do not bring a warm party spirit into a ... conversation which is designed for mutual improvement in the search of truth.** Take heed of allowing yourself in those self-satisfied assurances which keep the doors of the understanding barred fast against the admission of any new sentiments. Let your soul be ever ready to hearken to further discoveries, from a constant and ruling consciousness of

our ... fallible and imperfect state; and make it appear to your friends, that it is no hard task for you to learn and pronounce those little words, "I was mistaken," how hard soever it be for the bulk of mankind to pronounce them.

(22) As you may sometimes raise inquiries for your own instruction and improvement, and draw out the learning, wisdom, and fine sentiments of your friends, who perhaps may be too reserved or modest, so at other times, **if you perceive a person unskilful in the matter of debate**, you may, by questions aptly proposed in the Socratic method (*see Appendix B*), **lead him into a clearer knowledge of the subject**: then you become his instructor, in such a manner as may not appear to make yourself his superior.

(23) **Take heed of affecting always to shine in company above the rest**, and to display the riches of your own understanding or your oratory, as though you would render yourself admirable to all that are present. This is seldom well taken in polite company; much less should you use such forms of speech as should insinuate the ignorance or dulness of those with whom you converse.

(24) **Though you should not affect to flourish in a copious harangue and a diffusive style in company, yet neither should you rudely interrupt and reproach him that happens to use it: but** when he has done speaking, **reduce his sentiments into a more contracted form**; not with a show of correcting, but as one who is doubtful whether you hit upon his true sense or no. Thus matters may be brought more easily from a wild confusion into a single point, questions may be sooner determined, and difficulties more easily removed.

(25) **Be not so ready to charge ignorance, prejudice, and mistake upon others, as you are to suspect yourself of it**: and in order to shew how free you are from prejudices, learn to bear contradiction with patience: let it be easy to you to hear your own opinion strongly opposed, especially in matters which are doubtful and disputable, amongst men of sobriety and virtue. Give a patient hearing to arguments on all sides; otherwise, you give the company occasion to suspect that it is not the evidence of truth has led you into this opinion, but some lazy anticipation of judgment; some beloved presumption, some long and rash possession of a party scheme, in which you desire to rest undisturbed. If your assent has been

established upon just and sufficient grounds, why should you be afraid to let the truth be put to the trial of argument?

(26) **Banish utterly out of all conversation**, and especially out of all learned and intellectual conference, **every thing that tends to provoke passion or raise a fire in the blood.** Let no sharp language, no noisy exclamation, no sarcasms or biting jests be heard among you; no perverse or invidious consequences be drawn from each other's opinions, and imputed to the person: let there be no wilful perversion of another's meaning; no sudden seizure of a lapsed syllable to play upon it, nor any abused construction of an innocent mistake: suffer not your tongue to insult a modest opponent that begins to yield; let there be no crowing and triumph, even where there is evident victory on your side. All these things are enemies to friendship, and the ruin of free conversation. The impartial search of truth requires all calmness and serenity, all temper and candour: mutual instructions can never be attained in the midst of passion, pride, and clamour, unless we suppose, in the midst of such a scene, there is a loud and penetrating lecture read by both sides, on the folly and shameful infirmities of human nature.

(27) **Whensoever**, therefore, **any unhappy word shall arise in company**, that might give you a reasonable disgust, quash the rising resentment, be it ever so just, and **command** your soul and **your tongue into silence**, lest you cancel the hopes of all improvement for that hour, and transform the learned conversation into the mean and vulgar form of reproaches and railing. The man who began to break the peace in such a society, will fall under the shame and conviction of such a silent reproof, if he has any thing ingenuous about him. **If this should not be sufficient, let a grave admonition, or a soft and gentle turn of wit**, with an air of pleasantry, **give** the warm disputer **an occasion to stop the progress of his indecent fire**, if not to retract the indecency, and quench the flame.

(28) **Inure yourself to a candid and obliging manner in all your conversation**, and acquire the art of pleasing address, even when you teach, as well as when you learn, and when you oppose, as well as when you assert or prove. This degree of politeness is not to be attained without a diligent attention to such kind of directions as are here laid down, and a frequent exercise and practice of them.

(29) If you would know what sort of companions you should select for the cultivation and advantage of the mind, the general rule is, **choose such *companions* as,** by their brightness of parts, and their diligence in study, or by their superior advancement in learning, or peculiar excellency in any art, science, or accomplishment, divine or human, **may be capable of administering to your improvement;** and be sure to maintain and keep some due regard to their moral character always, lest while you wander in quest of intellectual gain, you fall into the contagion of . . . vice. No wise man would venture into a house infected with the plague, in order to see the finest collections of any virtuoso in Europe.

(30) **Nor is it every sober person of your acquaintance, no, nor every man of bright parts, or rich in learning, that is fit to engage in free conversation for the inquiry after truth.** Let a person have ever so illustrious talents, yet he is not a proper associate for such a purpose, **if he lie under any of the following infirmities:**

(a) If he be **exceedingly reserved**, and hath either no inclination to discourse, or no tolerable capacity of speech and language for the communication of his sentiments.

(b) If he be **haughty and proud** of his knowledge, imperious in his airs, and is always fond of imposing his sentiments on all the company.

(c) If he be **positive and dogmatical** in his own opinions, and will dispute to the end; if he will resist the brightest evidence of truth, rather than suffer himself to be overcome, or yield to the plainest and strongest reasonings.

(d) If he be one who always **affects to outshine all the company**, and delights to hear himself talk and flourish upon a subject, and make long harangues, while the rest must be all silent and attentive.

(e) If he be a person of a **whiffling and unsteady turn of mind**, who cannot keep close to a point of controversy, but wanders from it perpetually, and is always solicitous to say something, whether it be pertinent to the question or no.

(f) If he be **fretful and peevish**, and given to resentment upon all occasions; if he knows not how to bear contradiction, or is ready to take things in a wrong sense; if he is swift to feel a

supposed offence, or to imagine himself affronted, and then break out into a sudden passion, or retain silent and sullen wrath.

(g) If he **affect wit on all occasions**, and is full of his conceits and puns, quirks or quibbles, jests and repartees; these may agreeably entertain and animate an hour of mirth, but they have no place in the search after truth.

(h) If he carry always about him a sort of **craft, and cunning**, and disguise, and act rather like a spy than a friend. Have a care of such an one as will make an ill use of freedom in conversation, and immediately charge heresy upon you, when you happen to differ from those sentiments which authority or custom has established.

In short, you should avoid the man, in such select conversation, who practices any thing that is unbecoming the character of a sincere, free, and open searcher after truth.

Now, though you may pay all the relative duties of life to persons of these unhappy qualifications, and treat them with decency and love, so far as religion and humanity oblige you, yet take care of entering into a free debate on matters of truth or falsehood in their company, ... I confess, if a person of such a temper happens to judge and talk well on such a subject, you may hear him with attention, and derive what profit you can from his discourse; but he is by no means to be chosen for a free conference in matters of learning and knowledge.

(31) While I would persuade you to be aware of such persons, and abstain from too much freedom of discourse amongst them, it is very natural to infer that **you should watch against the working of these evil qualities in your own breast**, if you happen to be tainted with any of them yourself. Men of learning and ingenuity will justly avoid your acquaintance, when they find such an unhappy and unsocial temper prevailing in you.

(32) To conclude, **when you retire from company, then converse with yourself in solitude**, and inquire what you have learned for the improvement of your understanding, or for the rectifying *of* your inclinations, for the increase of your virtues, or the ameliorating *of* your conduct and behaviour in any future parts of life. If you have

seen some of your company candid, modest, humble in their manner, wise and sagacious, just and pious in their sentiments, polite and graceful as well as clear and strong in their expression, and universally acceptable and lovely in their behaviour, endeavour to impress the idea of all these upon your memory, and treasure them up for your imitation.

(a) If the laws of **reason, decency, and civility, have not been well observed amongst your associates, take notice of those defects for your own improvement**: and from every occurrence of this kind remark something to imitate or to avoid, in elegant, polite, and useful conversation. Perhaps you will find, that some persons present have really displeased the company, by an excessive and too visible an affectation to please, i.e. by giving loose to servile flattery or promiscuous praise; while others were as ready to oppose and contradict every thing that was said. Some have deserved just censure for a morose and affected taciturnity; and others have been anxious and careful lest their silence should be interpreted a want of sense, and therefore they have ventured to make speeches, though they had nothing to say which was worth hearing. Perhaps you will observe that one was ingenious in his thoughts, and bright in his language, but he was so topful of himself that he let it spill on all the company; that he spoke well indeed, but that he spoke too long, and did not allow equal liberty or time to his associates. You will remark that another was full charged, to let out his words before his friend had done speaking, or impatient of the least opposition to any thing he said. You will remember that some persons have talked at large, and with great confidence, of things which they understood not, and others counted every thing tedious and intolerable that was spoken upon subjects out of their sphere, and they would fain confine the conference entirely within the limits of their own narrow knowledge and study. The errors of conversation are almost infinite.

(b) **By a review of such irregularities** as these, **you may learn to avoid** those **follies** and pieces of ill conduct which spoil good conversation, or make it less agreeable and less useful; and by degrees you will acquire that delightful and easy manner of

address and behaviour in all useful correspondencies, which may render your company every where desired and beloved; and at the same time, among the best of your companions, you may make the highest improvement, in your own intellectual acquisitions, that the discourse of mortal creatures will allow,
...

- *Disputes* -

Under the general head of conversation for the improvement of the mind, we may rank the practice of disputing; that is, when two or more persons appear to maintain different sentiments, and defend their own, or oppose the other's opinion, in alternate discourse, by some methods of argument.

As these disputes often arise in good earnest, where the two contenders do really believe the different propositions which they support; so sometimes they are appointed as mere trials of skill in academies, or schools, by the students; sometimes they are practised, and that with apparent fervour, in courts of judicature by lawyers, in order to gain the fees of their different clients, while both sides perhaps are really of the same sentiment with regard to the cause which is tried.

In common conversation, disputes are often managed without any forms of regularity or order, and they turn to good or evil purposes, chiefly according to the temper of the disputants. They may sometimes be successful to search out truth, sometimes effectual to maintain truth, and convince the mistaken; but at other times a dispute is a mere scene of battle in order to *achieve* victory and vain triumph.

There are some few general rules which should be observed in all debates whatsoever, if we would find out truth by them, or convince a friend of his error, even though they be not managed according to any settled forms of disputation: and as there are almost as many opinions and judgments of things as there are persons, so when several persons happen to meet and confer together upon any subject, they are ready to declare their different sentiments, and support them by such reasonings as they are capable of. This is called debating, or disputing, as is above described.

(1) **When persons begin a debate, they should always take care that they are agreed in some general principles or propositions,** which either more nearly or remotely affect the question in hand; for

otherwise they have no foundation or hope of convincing each other; they must have some common ground to stand upon, while they maintain the contest.

(2) When they find they agree in some remote propositions, then **let them search farther, and inquire how near they approach to each other's sentiments; and whatsoever propositions they agree in,** let these lay a foundation for the mutual hope of conviction. Hereby you will be prevented from running at every turn to some original and remote propositions and axioms, which practice both entangles and prolongs a dispute. . . .

(3) **The question should be cleared from all doubtful terms and needless additions;** and all things that belong to the question should be expressed in plain and intelligible language. This is so necessary a thing, that without it men will be exposed to . . . ridiculous contests . . .

(4) And not only the sense and meaning of the words used in the question should be settled and adjusted between the disputants, but **the precise point of inquiry should be distinctly fixed;** the question in debate should be limited precisely to its special extent, or declared to be taken in its more general sense. . . .

It is this trifling humour or dishonest artifice of changing the question, and wandering away from the first point of debate, which gives endless length to disputes, and causes both disputants to part without any satisfaction. And one chief occasion of it is this: when one of the combatants feels his cause run low and fail, and is just ready to be confuted and demolished, he is tempted to step aside to avoid the blow, and betakes him to a different question: thus, if his adversary be not well aware of him, he begins to entrench himself in a new fastness, and holds out the siege with a new artillery of thoughts and words. It is the pride of man which is the spring of this evil, and an unwillingness to yield up their own opinions even to be overcome by truth itself.

(5) Keep this always therefore upon your mind as an everlasting rule of conduct in your debates to find out truth, that **a resolute design,** or even a warm affectation **of victory, is the bane of all real improvement,** and an effectual bar against the admission of the truth which you profess to seek. This works with a secret, but a

powerful and mischievous influence in every dispute, unless we are much upon our guard. It appears in frequent conversation; every age, every sex, and each party of mankind are so fond of being in the right, that they know not how to renounce this unhappy prejudice, this vain love of victory.

When truth with bright evidence is ready to break in upon a disputant, and to overcome his objections and mistakes, how swift and ready is the mind to engage wit and fancy, craft and subtlety, to cloud and perplex and puzzle the truth, if possible? How eager is he to throw in some impertinent question to divert from the main subject? How swift to take hold of some occasional word, thereby to lead the discourse off from the point in hand? So much afraid is human nature of parting with its errors, and being overcome by truth. Just thus a hunted hare calls up all the shifts that nature hath taught her: she treads back her mazes, crosses and confounds her former track, and uses all possible methods to divert the scent, when she is in danger of being seized and taken. ... Would one imagine that any rational being should take such pains to avoid truth, and to escape the improvement of its understanding?

(6) When you come to a dispute in order to find out truth, do not presume that you are certainly possessed of it before-hand. **Enter the debate with a sincere design of yielding to reason, on which side soever it appears.** Use no subtle arts to cloud and entangle the question; hide not yourself in doubtful words and phrases; do not affect little shifts and subterfuges to avoid the force of an argument; take a generous pleasure to espy the first rising beams of truth, though it be on the side of your opponent; endeavour to remove the little obscurities that hang about it, and suffer and encourage it to break out into open and convincing light; that while your opponent perhaps may gain the better of your reasonings, yet you yourself may triumph over error; and I am sure that is a much more valuable acquisition and victory.

(7) **Watch narrowly in every dispute, that your opponent does not lead you unwarily to grant some principle of the proposition,** which will bring with it a fatal consequence, and lead you insensibly into his sentiment, **though it be far astray from the truth**; and by this wrong step you will be, as it were, plunged into dangerous errors before you are aware. ...

Remember this short and plain caution of the subtle errors of men. Let a snake but once thrust in his head at some small unguarded fold of your garment, and he will insensibly and unavoidably wind his whole body into your bosom, and give you a pernicious wound.

(8) On the other hand, when you have found your opponent **make any such concession as may turn to your real advantage in maintaining the truth**, be wise and watchful to observe it, and make a happy improvement of it. . . . .

(9) **When you are engaged in a dispute with a person of very different principles from yourself**, and you cannot find any ready way to prevail with him to embrace the truth by principles which you both freely acknowledge, **you may fairly make use of his own principles to shew him his mistake**, and thus convince or silence him from his own concessions. . . .

(10) Yet **great care must be taken, lest your debates break in upon your passions**, and awaken them to take part in the controversy. When the opponent pushes hard, and gives just and mortal wounds to our own opinions, our passions are very apt to feel the strokes, and to rise in resentment and defence. Self is so mingled with the sentiments which we have chosen, and has such a tender feeling of all the opposition which is made to them, that personal brawls are very ready to come in as seconds, to succeed and finish the dispute of opinions. Then noise, and clamour, and folly, appear in all their shapes, and chase reason and truth out of sight.

How unhappy is the case of frail and wretched mankind in this dark or dusky state of strong passion and glimmering reason? How ready are we, when our passions are engaged in the dispute, to consider more what loads of nonsense and reproach we can lay upon our opponent, than what reason and 'truth require in the controversy itself? Dismal are the consequences mankind are too often involved in by this evil principle; it is this common and dangerous practice that carries the heart aside from all that is fair and honest in our search after truth, or the propagation of it in the world. . . .

- *Formal Types of Disputation* -

These general directions are necessary, or at least useful, in all debates whatsoever, whether they arise in occasional conversation, or are appointed at any certain time or place; whether they are managed with or without any formal rules to govern them. But there are three sorts of disputation in which there are some forms and orders observed, and which are distinguished by these three names, viz. Socratic, Forensic, and Academic, i.e., the disputes of the schools.

Concerning each of these it may not be improper to discourse a little, and give a few particular directions or remarks about them. *See Appendix B.*

Chapter 8

STUDY OR MEDITATION

It has been ... established in some of the foregoing chapters, that neither our own observations, nor our reading the labours of the learned, nor the attendance on the best lectures of instruction, nor enjoying the brightest conversation, can ever make a man truly knowing and wise, without the labours of his own reason in surveying, examining, and judging concerning all subjects upon the best evidence he can acquire. A good genius, or sagacity of thought, and happy judgment, a capacious memory, and large opportunities of observation and converse, will do much of themselves towards the cultivation of the mind, where they are well improved; but where, to the advantage of learned lectures, living instructions, and well chosen books, diligence and study are superadded, this man has all human aids concurring to raise him to a superior degree of wisdom and knowledge.

Under the preceding heads of discourse it has been already declared how our own meditation and reflection should examine, cultivate, and improve all other methods and advantages of enriching the understanding. What remains in this chapter is to give some further occasional hints how to employ our own thoughts, what sort of subjects we should meditate on, and in what manner we should regulate our studies, and how we may improve our judgement, so as in the most effectual and compendious way to attain such knowledge as may be most useful for every man in his circumstances of life, and particularly for those of the learned professions.

(1) The first direction for youth is this, **learn betimes to distinguish between words and things**. Get clear and plain ideas of the things you are set to study. Do not content yourselves with mere words and names, lest your laboured improvements only amass a heap of

unintelligible phrases, and you feed upon husks instead of kernels.
...

(2) **Let not young students** apply themselves to **search out** deep, dark, and abstruse matters **far above their reach**, or spend their labour in any peculiar subjects, for which they have not the advantages of necessary antecedent learning, or books, or observations. Let them not be too hasty to know things above their present powers, nor plunge their inquiries at once into the depths of knowledge, nor begin to study any science in the middle of it; this will confound rather than enlighten the understanding; such practices may happen to discourage and jade the mind by an attempt above its power; it may balk the understanding, and create an aversion to future diligence, and perhaps by despair may forbid the pursuit of that subject for ever afterwards: as a limb overstrained by lifting a weight above its power, may never recover its former agility and vigour; or if it does, the man may be frighted from ever exerting its strength again.

(3) **Nor yet let any student**, on the other hand, **fright himself at every turn with insurmountable difficulties**, nor imagine that the truth is wrapt up in impenetrable darkness. These are formidable spectres which the understanding raises sometimes to flatter its own laziness. Those things which in a remote and confused view seem very obscure and perplexed, may be approached by gentle and regular steps, and may then unfold and explain themselves at large to the eye. The hardest problems in geometry, and the most intricate schemes or diagrams, may be explicated and understood, step by step: ...

(4) **In learning any new thing, there should be as little as possible first proposed to the mind at once**, and that being understood and fully mastered, proceed then to the next adjoining part yet unknown. This is a slow, but safe and sure way to arrive at knowledge. If the mind apply itself at first to easier subjects, and things near akin to what is already known, and then advance to the more remote and knotty parts of knowledge by slow degrees, it would be able in this manner to cope with great difficulties, and prevail over them with amazing and happy success. ...

(5) **Engage not the mind in the intense pursuit of too many things at once**; especially such as have no relation to one another. This will

be ready to distract the understanding, and hinder it from attaining perfection in any one subject of study. Such a practice gives a slight smattering of several sciences, without any solid and substantial knowledge of them, and without any real and valuable improvement; and though two or three sorts of study may be usefully carried on at once, to entertain the mind with variety, that it may not be overtired with one sort of thoughts, yet a multitude of subjects will too much distract the attention, and weaken the application of the mind to any one of them.

(6) **Where two or three sciences are pursued at the same time, if one of them be dry**, abstracted, and unpleasant, as logic, metaphysics, law, languages, **let another be more entertaining and agreeable, to secure the mind from weariness**, and aversion to study. Delight should be intermingled with labour as far as possible, to allure us to bear the fatigue of dry studies the better. Poetry, practical mathematics, history, etc. are generally esteemed entertaining studies, and may be happily used for this purpose. Thus while we relieve a dull and heavy hour by some alluring employments of the mind, our very diversions enrich our understandings, and our pleasure is turned into profit.

(7) In the pursuit of every valuable subject of knowledge, **keep the end always in your eye**, and be not diverted from it by every petty trifle you meet with in the way. Some persons have such a wandering genius that they are ready to pursue every incidental theme or occasional idea, till they have lost sight of their original subject. These are the men who, when they are engaged in conversation, prolong their story by dwelling on every incident, and swell their narrative with long parentheses, till they have lost their first designs; like a man who is sent in quest of some great treasure, but he steps aside to gather every flower he finds, or stands still to dig up every shining pebble he mets with in his way, till the treasure is forgotten and never found.

(8) **Exert your care, skill, and diligence, about every subject and every question, in just proportion to the importance of it**, together with the danger and bad consequences of ignorance or error therein. Many excellent advantages flow from this one direction:

> *(a)* This rule will teach you to **be very careful in gaining some general and fundamental truth** both in philosophy, religion,

and in human life; because they are of the highest moment, and conduct our thoughts with ease into a thousand inferior and particular propositions. . . .

We should be very curious in examining all propositions that pretend to this honour of being general principles: and we should not without just evidence admit into this rank mere matters of common fame, or commonly received opinions; no, nor the general determinations of the learned, or the established articles of any . . . nation, etc. for there are many learned presumptions, many synodical and national mistakes, many established falsehoods, as well as many vulgar errors, wherein multitudes of men have followed one another for whole ages almost blindfold. It is of great importance for every man to be careful that these general principles are just and true; for one error may lead us into thousands, which will naturally follow, if once a leading falsehood be admitted. . . .

(b) **In matters of practice we should be most careful to fix our end right**, and wisely determine the scope at which we aim, because that is to direct us in the choice and use of all the means to attain it. If our end be wrong, all our labour in the means will be in vain, or perhaps so much the more pernicious as they are better suited to attain that mistaken end. If mere sensible pleasure, or human grandeur, or wealth, be our chief end, we shall choose means contrary to piety and virtue, and proceed apace towards real misery. . . .

(c) This rule will make us solicitous not only to **avoid such** errors, whose influence will spread wide into the whole scheme of our own knowledge and practice, but such **mistakes** also **whose influence would be yet more extensive and injurious to others** as well as to ourselves: perhaps to many persons or many families, to a whole church, a town, a country, or a kingdom. Upon this account, persons who are called to instruct others, who are raised to any eminence either in church or state, ought to be careful in settling their principles in *civil and moral* matters, . . . lest a mistake of theirs should diffuse wide mischief, should draw along with it most pernicious consequences, and perhaps extend to following generations. . . .

(9) **Have a care lest some beloved notion, or some darling science, so far prevail over your mind as to give a sovereign tincture to all your other studies**, and discolour all your ideas, like a person in the jaundice, who spreads a yellow scene with his eyes all over the objects which he meets. ...

Under this influence ... some have been tempted to cast all their logical, their metaphysical, and their theological and moral learning into the method of mathematicians, and bring every thing relating to those abstracted, or those practical sciences, under theorems, problems, postulates, scholiums, corollaries, etc. whereas, the matter ought always to direct the method; for all subjects or matters of thought cannot be moulded or subdued to one form. Neither the rules for conduct of the understanding nor the doctrines nor duties of religion and virtue, can be exhibited naturally in figures and diagrams. Things are to be considered as they are in themselves; their natures are inflexible, and their natural relations unalterable; and therefore in order to conceive them aright, we must bring our understandings to things, and not pretend to bend and strain things to comport with our fancies and forms.

(10) **Suffer not any beloved study to prejudice your mind so far in favour of it as to despise all other learning.** This is a fault of some little souls, who have got a smattering of astronomy, chemistry, metaphysics, history, etc. and for want of a due acquaintance with other sciences make a scoff at them in all comparison of their favourite science. Their understandings are hereby cooped up in narrow bounds, so that they never look abroad into other provinces of the intellectual world, which are more beautiful, perhaps, and more fruitful than their own: if they would search a little into other sciences, they might not only find treasures of new knowledge, but might be furnished also with rich hints of thought, and glorious assistances to cultivate that very province to which they have confined themselves.

(11) **Let every particular study have due and proper time assigned it**, and let not a favourite science prevail with you to lay out such hours upon it, as ought to be employed upon the more necessary and more important affairs or studies of your profession. When you have, according to the best of your discretion, and according to the

circumstances of your life, fixed proper hours for particular studies, endeavour to keep to those rules; not indeed with a superstitious preciseness, but with some good degrees of a regular constancy. Order and method in a course of study saves much time, and makes large improvements. Such a fixation of certain hours will have a happy influence to secure you from trifling and wasting away your minutes in impertinence.

(12) **Do not apply yourself to any one study at one time longer than the mind is capable of giving a close attention to it without weariness or wandering.** Do not over-fatigue the spirits at any time, lest the mind be seized with a lassitude, and thereby be tempted to nauseate and grow tired of a particular subject before you have finished it.

(13) **In the beginning of your application to any new subject, be not too uneasy under present difficulties that occur,** nor too importunate and impatient for answers and solutions to any questions that arise. Perhaps a little more study, a little further acquaintance with the subject, a little time and experience will solve those difficulties, untie the knot, and make your doubts vanish: especially if you are under the instruction of a tutor, he can inform you that your inquiries are perhaps too early, and that you have not yet learned those principles upon which the solution of such a difficulty depends.

(14) **Do not expect to arrive at certainty in every subject which you pursue.** There are a hundred things wherein we ... must be content with probability, where our best light and reasonings will reach no further. We must balance arguments as justly as we can, and where we cannot find weight enough on either side to determine the scale with sovereign force and assurance, we must content ourselves perhaps with a small preponderation. This will give us a probable opinion, and those probabilities are sufficient for the daily determination of a thousand actions in human life, ...

It is admirably well expressed by a late writer, "When there is a great strength of argument set before us, if we will refuse to do what appears most fit for us, till every little objection is removed, we shall never take one wise resolution as long as we live."

(15) **Endeavour to apply every speculative study,** as far as possible, **to some practical use,** that both yourself and others may be the better

for it. Inquiries even in natural philosophy should not be mere amusements, . . . Researchers into the springs of natural bodies and their motions should lead men to invent happy methods for the ease and convenience of human life; . . .

If we pursue mathematical speculations, they will inure us to attend closely to any subject, to seek and gain clear ideas, to distinguish truth from falsehood, to judge justly, and to argue strongly; and these studies do more directly furnish us with all the various rules of those useful arts of life, viz. measuring, building, sailing, etc.

Even our very inquiries and disputations about vacuum or space, and atoms, about incommensurable quantities, and infinite divisibility of matter, and eternal duration, which seem to be purely speculative, will shew us some good practical lessons, will lead us to see the weakness of our nature, . . .

(16) Though we should always be ready to change our sentiments of things upon just conviction of their falsehood, yet there is not the same necessity of changing our accustomed methods of reading or study and practice, even though we have not been led at first in to the happiest method. Our thought may be true, though we may have hit upon an improper order of thinking. **Truth does not always depend upon the most convenient method.** There may be a certain form and order in which we have long accustomed ourselves to range our ideas and notions, which may be best for us now, though it was not originally best in itself. The inconveniences of changing may be much greater than the conveniences we could obtain by a new method.

Chapter 9

FIXING THE ATTENTION

A student should labour, by all proper methods, to acquire a steady fixation of thought. Attention is a very necessary thing in order to improve our minds. The evidence of truth does not always appear immediately, nor strike the soul at first sight. It is by long attention and inspection that we arrive at evidence, and it is for want of it we judge falsely of many things. We make haste to determine upon a slight and sudden view, we confirm our guesses which arise from a glance, we pass a judgment while we have but a confused or obscure perception, and thus plunge ourselves into mistakes. This is like a man who walking in a mist, or being at a great distance from any visible object, (suppose a tree, a man, a horse, or a church), judges much amiss of the figure, and situation, and colours of it, and sometimes takes one for the other; whereas, if he would but withold his judgment till he came nearer to it, or stay till clearer light comes, and then would fix his eyes longer upon it, he would secure himself from those mistakes.

Now, in order to gain a greater facility of attention, we may observe these rules:

(1) **Get a good liking to the study or knowledge you would pursue.** We may observe, that there is not much difficulty in confining the mind to contemplate what we have a great desire to know; and especially if they are matters of sense, or ideas which paint themselves upon the fancy. It is but acquiring an hearty good-will and resolution to search out and survey the various properties and parts of such objects, and our attention will be engaged, if there be any delight or diversion in the study or contemplation of them. Therefore mathematical studies have a strange influence towards fixing the attention of the mind, and giving a steadiness to a wandering

disposition, because they deal much in lines, figures, and numbers, which affect and please the sense and imagination. Histories have a strong tendency the same way, for they engage the soul by a variety of sensible occurrences; when it hath begun, it knows not how to leave off; it longs to know the final event, through a natural curiosity that belongs to mankind. Voyages and travels, and accounts of strange countries and strange appearances, will assist in this work. This sort of study detains the mind by the perpetual occurrence and expectation of something new, and that which may gratefully strike the imagination.

(2) **Sometimes we may make use of sensible things and corporeal images for the illustration of those notions which are more abstracted and intellectual.** Therefore diagrams greatly assist the mind in astronomy and philosophy; and the emblems of virtues and vices may happily teach children, and pleasingly impress those useful moral ideas on young minds, which perhaps might be conveyed to them with much more difficulty by mere moral and abstracted discourses.

I confess, in this practice of representing moral subjects by pictures, we should be cautious lest we so far immerse the mind in corporeal images, as to render it unfit to take in an abstracted and intellectual idea, or cause it to form wrong conceptions of immaterial things. This practice, therefore, is rather to be used at first in order to get a fixed habit of attention, and in some cases only; but it can never be our constant way and method of pursuing all moral, abstracted, and spiritual themes.

(3) **Apply yourself to those studies, and read those authors who draw out their subjects into a perpetual chain of connected reasonings,** wherein the following parts of the discourse are naturally and easily derived from those which go before. Several of the mathematical sciences, if not all, are happily useful for this purpose. This will render the labour of study delightful to a rational mind, and will fix the powers of the understanding with strong attention to their proper operations by the very pleasure of it. . . .

(4) **Do not choose your constant place of study by the finery of the prospects, or the most various and entertaining scenes of sensible things.** Too much light, or a variety of objects which strike the eye or the ear, especially while they are ever in motion or often

changing, have a natural and powerful tendency to steal away the mind too often from its steady pursuit of any subject which we contemplate; and thereby the soul gets a habit of silly curiosity and impertinence, of trifling and wandering. ...

(5) **Be not in too much haste to come to the determination of a difficult or important point.** Think it worth your waiting to find out truth. Do not give your assent up to either side of a question too soon, merely on this account, that the study of it is long and difficult. Rather be contented with ignorance for a season, and continue in suspense till your attention, and meditation, and due labour, have found out sufficient evidence on one side. Some are so fond to know a great deal at once, and love to talk of things with freedom and boldness before they truly understand them, that they scarcely ever allow themselves attention enough to search the matter through and through.

(6) **Have a care of indulging the more sensual passions and appetites of animal nature; they are great enemies to attention.** Let not the mind of a student be under the influence of any warm affection to things of sense, when he comes to engage in the search of truth, or the improvement of his understanding. A person under the power of love, or fear, or anger, great pain, or deep sorrow, hath so little government of his soul, that he cannot keep it attentive to the proper subject of his meditation. The passions call away the thoughts with incessant importunity towards the object that excited them; and if we indulge the frequent rise and roving of passions, we shall thereby procure an unsteady and unattentive habit of mind.

Yet this one exception must be admitted, viz. If we can be so happy as to engage any passion of the soul on the side of the particular study which we are pursuing, it may have great influence to fix the attention more strongly to it. ...

Chapter 10

ENLARGING THE CAPACITY OF THE MIND

There are three things which in an especial manner go to make up that amplitude or capacity of mind which is one of the noblest characters belonging to the understanding. . . .

(1) . . . **An ample and capacious mind which is ready to take in vast and sublime ideas without pain or difficulty.** Persons who have never been used to converse with any thing but the common, little, and obvious affairs of life, have acquired such a narrow or contracted habit of soul, that they are not able to stretch their intellects wide enough to admit large and noble thoughts; they are ready to make their domestic, daily, and familiar images of things the measure of all that is, and all that can be. . . .

(2) . . . When **the mind is free to receive new and strange ideas and propositions upon just evidence without any great surprise or aversion.** Those who confine themselves within the circle of their own hereditary ideas and opinions, and who never give themselves leave so much as to examine or believe any thing beside the dictates of their own family, or sect, or party, are justly charged with a narrowness of soul.

(3) . . . **An ability to receive many ideas at once without confusion.** The ample mind takes a survey of several objects with one glance, keeps them all within sight and present to the soul, and they may be compared together in their mutual respects; it forms just judgments, and it draws proper inferences from this comparison, even to a great length of argument, and a chain of demonstrations.

The narrowness that belongs to human souls in general is a great imperfection and impediment to wisdom and happiness. There are but few persons who can contemplate or practise several things at once; our faculties are very limited, and while we are intent upon one part or property of a subject, we have but a slight glimpse of the rest, or we lose it out of sight. But it is a sign of a large and capacious mind, if we can with one single view take in a variety of objects; or at least when the mind can apply itself to several objects with so swift a succession, and in so few moments, as attains almost the same ends as if it were all done in the same instant.

This is a necessary qualification in order to *attain* great knowledge and good judgment; for there are several things in human life, ... and in the sciences, which have various circumstances, appendices, and relations attending them; and without a survey of all those ideas which stand in connexion with and relation to each other, we are often in danger of passing a false judgment on the subject proposed. It is for this reason there are so numerous controversies found among the learned and unlearned world ... in the affairs of civil government.

It is owing to the narrowness of our minds that we are exposed to the same peril in the matters of human duty and prudence. In many things which we do, we ought not only to consider the mere naked action itself, but the persons who act, the persons towards whom, the time when, the place where, the manner how, the end for which the action is done, together with the effects that must or may follow, and all other surrounding circumstances; these things must necessarily be taken into our view, in order to determine whether the action, which is indifferent in itself, be either lawful or unlawful, good or evil, wise or foolish, decent or indecent, proper or improper, as it is so circumstantiated.

Let me give a plain instance for the illustration of this matter. Mario kills a dog, which, considered merely in itself, seems to be an indifferent action: now the dog was Timon's, and not his own; this makes it look unlawful. But Timon bid him do it; this gives it an appearance of lawfulness again. It was done at church, and in time of divine service; these circumstances added, cast on it an air of irreligion. But the dog flew at Mario, and put him in danger of his life; this relieves the seeming impiety of the action. Yet Mario might have escaped by flying thence; therefore the action appears to be improper. But the dog was known to be mad; this further circumstance makes it almost necessary that the dog should be slain, lest he might worry the assembly, and do much mischief. Yet again, Mario killed with a pistol, which he happened to have in his pocket since yesterday's journey; now hereby the whole congregation was terrified and discomposed, and divine service was broken off: this carries an appearance of great indecency and impropriety in it: but after all, when we consider a further circumstance, that Mario, being thus violently assaulted by a mad dog, had no way of escape, and had no other weapon about him, it seems to take away all the colours of impropriety, indecency, or unlawfulness, and to allow that the preservation of one or many lives will justify the act as wise and good. Now all these concurrent appendices of the action ought to be surveyed, in order to pronounce with justice and truth concerning it. ...

Whence by the way I may take occasion to say, how many thousands are there who take upon them to pass their censures on the personal and the domestic actions of others, who pronounce boldly on the affairs of the public, and determine the justice or madness, the wisdom or folly of national administrations, of peace and war, etc. ... They were not capable of entering into the numerous concurring springs of action, nor had they ever taken a survey of the twentieth part of the circumstances which were necessary for such judgments or censures.

It is the narrowness of our minds, as well as the vices of the will, that oftentimes prevents us from taking a full view of all the complicated and concurring appendices that belong to human actions: thence it comes to pass that there is so little right judgment, so little justice, prudence, or decency, practiced among the bulk of mankind; thence arise infinite reproaches and censures, alike foolish and unrighteous. You see, therefore, how needful and happy a thing it is to be possessed of some measure of this amplitude of soul, in order to make us very wise, or knowing, or just, or prudent, or happy.

I confess this sort of amplitude or capacity of mind is in a great measure the gift of nature, for some are born with much more capacious souls than others.

The genius of some persons is so poor and limited, that they can hardly take in the connexion of two or three propositions, unless it be in matters of sense, and which they have learned by experience:

they are utterly unfit for speculative studies; it is hard for them to discern the difference betwixt right and wrong in matters of reason on any abstracted subjects; these ought never to set up for scholars, but apply themselves to those arts and professions of life which are to be learned at an easier rate, by slow degrees and daily experience.

Others have a soul a little more capacious, and they can take in the connexion of a few propositions pretty well; but if the chain of consequences be a little prolix, here they stick and are confounded. If persons of this make ever devote themselves to science, they should be well assured of a solid and strong constitution of body, and well resolved to bear the fatigue of hard labour and diligence in study: if the iron be bent, King Solomon tells us, we must put more strength.

But, in the third place, there are some of so bright and happy a genius, and so ample a mind, that they can take in a long train of propositions, if not at once, yet in a very few moments, and judge well concerning the dependence of them. They can survey a variety of complicated ideas without fatigue or disturbance; and a number of truths offering themselves as it were in one view to their understanding, doth not perplex or confound them. This makes a great man.

- *Rules* -

Now, though there may be much owing to nature in ... *these cases*, yet experience assures us, that even a lower degree of this capacity and extent of thought may be increased by diligence and application, by frequent exercise, and the observation of such rules as these:

(1) **Labour by all means to gain an attentive and patient temper of mind**, a power of confining and fixing your thoughts so long on any one appointed subject, till you have surveyed it on every side and in every situation, and run through the several powers, parts, properties and relations, effects and consequences of it. He whose thoughts are very fluttering and wandering, and cannot be fixed attentively to a few ideas successively, will never be able to survey many and various objects distinctly at once, but will certainly be overwhelmed and confounded with the multiplicity of them. The rules for fixing the attention in the former chapter are proper to be consulted here.

(2) **Accustom yourself to clear and distinct ideas in every thing you think of.** Be not satisfied with obscure and confused conceptions of things, especially where clearer may be obtained: for one obscure or confused idea, especially if it be of great importance in the question, intermingled with many clear ones, and placed in its variety of aspects towards them, will be in danger of spreading confusion over the whole scene of ideas, and thus may have an unhappy influence to overwhelm the understanding with darkness and pervert the judgment. A little black paint will shamefully tincture and spoil twenty gay colours.

Consider yet further, that if you content yourself frequently with words instead of ideas, or with cloudy and confused notions of things, how impenetrable will that darkness be, and how vast and endless that confusion, which must surround and involve the understanding, when many of these obscure and confused ideas come to be set before the soul at once? ...

(3) **Use all diligence to acquire and treasure up a large store of ideas and notions**: take every opportunity to add something to your stock; and by frequent recollection fix them in your memory: nothing tends to confirm and enlarge the memory like a frequent review of its possessions. Then the brain being well furnished with various traces, signatures, and images, will have a rich treasure always ready to be proposed or offered to the soul, when it directs its thought towards any particular subject. This will gradually give the mind a faculty of surveying many objects at once, as a room that is richly adorned and hung round with a great variety of pictures strokes the eye almost at once with all that variety, especially if they have been well surveyed one by one at first: this makes it habitual and more easy to the inhabitants to take in many of those painted scenes with a single glance or two.

Here note, that by acquiring a rich treasure of notions, I do not mean only single ideas, but also propositions, observations, and experiences, with reasonings and arguments upon the various subjects that occur among natural and moral, common or sacred affairs; that when you are called to judge concerning any question, you will have some principles of truth, some useful axioms and observations, always ready at hand to direct and assist your judgment.

(4) It is necessary that we should as far as possible **entertain and lay up our daily new ideas in a regular order**, and range the acquisitions of our souls under proper heads, whether of divinity, law, physics, mathematics, morality, politics, trade, domestic life, civility, decency, etc. whether of cause, effect, substance, mode, power, property, body, spirit, etc. We should inure our minds to method and order continually; and when we take in any fresh ideas, occurrences, and observations, we should dispose of them in their proper places, and see how they stand and agree with the rest of our notions on the same subjects: as a scholar would dispose of a new book on a proper shelf among its kindred authors; or as an officer at the post-house in London disposes of every letter he takes in, placing it in the box that belongs to the proper road or county.

In any of these cases, if things lay all in a heap, the addition of any new object would increase the confusion; but method gives a speedy and short survey of them with ease and pleasure. Method is of admirable advantage to keep our ideas from a confused mixture, and to preserve them ready for every use. The science of ontology which distributes all beings, and all the affections of being, whether absolute or relative, under proper classes, is of good service to keep our intellectual acquisitions in such order as that the mind may survey them at once.

(5) As method is necessary for the improvement of the mind, in order to make your treasure of ideas most useful, so in all your further pursuits of truth and acquirements of rational knowledge, **observe a regular progressive method**. Begin with the most simple, easy, and obvious ideas; then by degrees join two, and three, and more of them together: thus the complicated ideas growing up under your eye and observation, will not give the same confusion of thought as they would do if they were all offered to the mind at once, without your observing the original and formation of them. An eminent example of this appears in the study of arithmetic. If a scholar just admitted into the school observes his master performing an operation in the rule of division, his head is at once disturbed and confounded with the manifold comparisons of the numbers of the divisor and dividend, and the multiplication of the one and subtraction of it from the other; but if he begin regularly at addition, and so proceed by subtraction and multiplication, he

will then in a few weeks be able to take in an intelligent survey of all those operations in division, and to practice them himself with ease and pleasure, each of which at first seemed all intricacy and confusion. . . .

But this advantage does not belong only to mathematical learning. If we apply ourselves at first in any science to clear and single ideas, and never hurry ourselves on to the following and more complicated parts of knowledge, till we thoroughly understand the foregoing, we may practice the same method of enlarging the capacity of the soul with success in any one of the sciences, or in the affairs of life . . .

Beginning with A, B, C, and making syllables out of letters, and words out of syllables, has been the foundation of all that glorious superstructure of arts and sciences which have enriched the minds and libraries of the learned world in several ages. These are the first steps by which the ample and capacious souls among mankind have arrived at that prodigious extent of knowledge, which renders them the wonder and glory of the nation where they live. Though Plato and Cicero, Descartes and Mr. Boyle, Mr. Locke and Sir Isaac Newton, were doubtless favoured by nature with a genius of uncommon amplitude; yet, in their early years, and first attempts of sciences, this was but limited and narrow, in comparison of what they attained at last. But how vast and capacious were those powers which they afterwards acquired by patient attention and watchful observation, by the pursuit of clear ideas and a regular method of thinking!

Chapter 11

IMPROVING THE MEMORY

Memory is a distinct faculty of the mind of man, very different from perception, judgment, and reasoning, and its other powers. ... We are said to remember any thing when the idea of it arises in the mind with a consciousness at the same time that we have had this idea before. Our memory is our natural power of retaining what we learn, and of recalling it on every occasion. Therefore we can never be said to remember any thing, whether it be ideas or propositions, words or things, notions or arguments, of which we have not had some former idea or perception either by sense or imagination, thought or reflection; but whatsoever we learn from observation, books, or conversation, etc. it must all be laid up and preserved in the memory, if we would make it really useful.

... Without memory the soul of man would be but a poor, destitute, naked being, with an everlasting blank spread over it, except the fleeting ideas of the present moment.

Memory is very useful to those who speak as well as to those who learn; it assists the teacher and the orator, as well as the scholar or the hearer. The best speeches and instructions are almost lost, if those who hear them immediately forget them. And those who are called to speak in public are much better heard and accepted, when they can deliver their discourse by the help of a lively genius and a ready memory, than when they are forced to read all that they would communicate to their hearers. Reading is certainly a heavier way of the conveyance of our sentiments; and there are very few mere readers who have the felicity of penetrating the soul, and awakening the passions of those who hear, by such a grace and power of oratory, as the man who seems to talk every word from his very heart, and pours out the riches of his own knowledge upon the people round about him by the help of a free and copious memory. This gives life and spirit to every thing that is spoken, and has a natural tendency to make a deeper impression on the minds of men: it awakens the dullest spirits, causes them to receive a discourse with more affection and pleasure, and adds a singular grace and excellency both to the person and his oration.

A good judgment and a good memory are very different qualifications. A person may have a very strong, capacious, and retentive memory, where the judgment is very poor and weak: as sometimes it happens in those who are but one degree above an idiot, who have manifested an amazing strength and extent of memory, but have hardly been able to join or disjoin two or three ideas in a wise and happy manner to make a solid, rational proposition.

There have been instances of others who have had but a very tolerable power of memory, yet their judgment has been of a much superior degree, just and wise, solid and excellent.

... A good judgment must always in some measure depend upon a survey and comparison of several things together in the mind, and determining the truth of some doubtful proposition by that survey and comparison. ... Now there can be no such comprehensive survey of many things without a tolerable degree of memory; it is by reviewing things past we learn to judge of the future: and it happens sometimes that if one needful or important object or idea be absent, the judgment concerning the thing inquired will thereby become false or mistaken. ...

Where the memory has been almost constantly employing itself in scraping together new acquirements, and where there has not been a judgment sufficient to distinguish what things were fit to be recommended and treasured up in the memory, and what things were idle, useless, or needless, the mind has been filled with a wretched heap and hotch-potch of words or ideas, and the soul may be said to have had large possessions, but no true riches.

A good memory has these several qualifications.

- It is ready to receive and admit, with great ease, the various ideas both of words and things which are learned or taught.
- It is large and copious to treasure up these ideas in great number and variety.
- It is strong and durable to retain for a considerable time those words or thoughts which are committed to it.

- It is faithful and active to suggest and recollect, upon every proper occasion, all those words or thoughts which have been recommended to its care, or treasured up in it. . . .

There is one great and general direction which belongs to the improvement of other powers as well as of the memory, and that is, to keep it always in due and proper exercise. Many acts by degrees form a habit, and thereby the ability or power is strengthened, and made more ready to appear again in action. Our memories should be used and inured from childhood to bear a moderate quantity of knowledge let into them early, and they will thereby become strong for use and service. . . .

Our memories will be in a great measure moulded and formed, improved or injured, according to the exercise of them. If we never use them, they will be almost lost. Those who are wont to converse or read about a few things only, will retain but a few in their memory: those who are used to remember things but for an hour, and charge their memories with it no longer, will retain them but an hour before they vanish. . . .

. . . Teachers should wisely judge of the power and constitution of youth, and impose no more on them than they are able to bear with cheerfulness and improvement.

And particularly they should take care that the memory of the learner be not too much crowded with a tumultuous heap or overbearing multitude of documents or ideas at one time; this is the way to remember nothing: one idea effaces another. An over-greedy grasp does not retain the largest handful. But it is the exercise of memory with a due moderation, that is one general rule towards the improvement of it.

- Rules -

The particular rules are such as these:

(1) **Due attention and diligence to learn and know things which we would commit to our remembrance,** is a rule of great necessity in this case. When the attention is strongly fixed to any particular subject, all that is said concerning it makes a deeper impression upon the mind. There are some persons who complain they cannot remember . . . human discourses which they hear, when in truth their thoughts are wandering half the time, or they hear with such coldness and indifferency, and a trifling temper of spirit, that it is no wonder the things which are read or spoken make but a slight

impression on the brain, and get no firm footing in the seat of memory, but soon vanish and are lost.

It is needful, therefore, if we would maintain a long remembrance of the things which we read or hear, that we should engage our delight and pleasure in those subjects, and use the other methods which are before prescribed in order to fix the attention. Sloth, indolence, and idleness, will no more bless the mind with intellectual riches, than it will fill the hand with gain, the field with corn, or the purse with treasure. ...

(2) Clear and distinct apprehension of the things which we commit to memory, is necessary in order to make them stick and dwell there. If we would remember words, or learn the names of persons or things, we should have them recommended to our memory by a clear and distinct pronunciation, spelling, or writing. If we would treasure up the ideas of things, notions, propositions, arguments, and sciences, these should be recommended also to our memory by a clear and distinct perception of them. Faint, glimmering, and confused ideas, will vanish like images seen in twilight. **Every thing which we learn should be conveyed to the understanding in the plainest expressions, without any ambiguity**, that we may not mistake what we desire to remember. This is a general rule, whether we would employ the memory about words or things, though it must be confest that mere sounds and words are much harder to get by heart than the knowledge of things and real images.

(a) For this reason **take heed** (as I have often before warned) that **you do not take up with words instead of things, nor** mere **sounds instead of** real **sentiments and ideas**. Many a lad forgets what has been taught him, merely because he never well understood it; he never clearly and distinctly took in the meaning of those sounds and syllables which he was required to get by heart.

(3) **Method and regularity in the things we commit to memory**, is necessary in order to make them take more effectual possession of the mind, and abide there long. ...

(a) **Whatsoever you would trust to your memory, let it be disposed in a proper method, connected well together, and referred to distinct and particular heads or classes**, both general and

particular. An apothecary's boy will much sooner learn all the medicines in his master's shop, when they are ranged in boxes or on shelves according to their distinct natures, ...

(b) **The mutual dependence of things on each other help the memory of both.** A wise connection of the parts of a discourse in a rational method, gives great advantage to the reader or hearer ... *for* his remembrance of it. Therefore many mathematical demonstrations in a long train may be remembered much better than a heap of sentences which have no connection. ...

(4) **A frequent review, and careful repetition of the things we would learn,** and an abridgement of them in a narrow compass for this end, has a great influence to fix them in the memory: therefore it is that the rules of grammar, and useful examples of the variation of words, and the peculiar forms of speech in any language, are so often appointed by the masters as lessons for the scholars to be frequently repeated; and they are contracted into tables for frequent review, that what is not fixed in the mind at first, may be stamped upon the memory by a perpetual survey and rehearsal.

Repetition is so very useful a practice, ... never read a book without making some small points, dashes ... in the margin to mark what parts of the discourse *are* proper for a review ...

(a) **Even when a person is hearing ... a lecture, he may give his thoughts leave now and then to step back so far as to recollect the several heads of it from the beginning,** two or three times before the lecture ... is finished: the omission or the loss of a sentence or two among the amplifications is richly compensated by preserving in the mind the method and order of the whole discourse in the most important branches of it.

(b) **If we would fix in the memory the discourses we hear,** or what we design to speak, **let us abstract them into brief compends, and review them often.** Lawyers ... have need of such assistances: they write down short notes or hints of the principal heads of what they desire to commit to their memory in order to ... plead, for such abstracts and epitomes may be reviewed much sooner, and the several amplifying sentiments or sentences will be more easily invented or recollected in their

proper places. The art of short hand is of excellent use for this as well as for other purposes. It must be acknowledged, that those who scarcely ever take a pen in their hand to write short notes or hints of what they are to speak or learn, who never try to cast things into method, or to contract the survey of them in order to commit them to their memory, . . . need *to* have a double degree of that natural power of retaining and recollecting what they read, or hear, or intend to speak.

(c) **Do not plunge yourself into other businesses or studies, amusements or recreations, immediately after you have attended upon instruction,** if you can well avoid it. Get time if possible to recollect the things you have heard, that they may not be washed all away from the mind by a torrent of other occurrences or engagements, nor lost in the crowd or clamour of other loud or importunate affairs.

(d) **Talking over the things which you have read with your companions** on the first proper opportunity you have for it, **is a most useful manner of review or repetition**, in order to fix them upon the mind. Teach them *to* your younger friends, in order to establish your own knowledge while you communicate it to them. The animal powers of your tongue and of your ear, as well as your intellectual faculties, will all join together to help the memory. . . .

(5) **Pleasure and delight in the things we learn, give great assistance towards the remembrance of them.** Whatsoever therefore we desire that a child should commit to his memory, make it as pleasant to him as possible; endeavour to search his genius and his temper, and let him take in the instructions you give him, or the lessons you appoint him, as far as may be, in a way suited to his natural inclination.

(6) **The memory of useful things may receive considerable aid if they are thrown into verse**: for the numbers and measures, and rhyme, according to the poesy of different languages, have a considerable influence upon mankind, both to make them receive with more ease the things proposed to their observation, and preserve them longer in their remembrance. How many are there of the common affairs of human life which have been taught in early years by the help of

rhyme, and have been like nails fastened in a sure place, and rivetted by daily use?

So the number of the days each month are engraven on the memory of thousands by these four lines:

> Thirty days hath September,
> June and April and November:
> February twenty-eight alone,
> And all the rest have thirty-one. . . .

(7) **When you would remember new things or words, endeavour to associate and connect them with some words or things which you have well known before**, and which are fixed and established in your memory. This association of ideas is of great importance and force, and may be of excellent use in many instances of human life. One idea which is familiar to the mind, connected with others which are new and strange, will bring those new ideas to easy remembrance. . . .

> *(a)* **It is also by this association of ideas that we may better imprint any new idea upon the memory, by joining with it some circumstance** of the time, place, company, etc. **wherein we first observed, heard, or learned it**. If we would recover an absent idea, it is useful to recollect those circumstances of time, place, etc. The substance will many times be recovered and brought to the thoughts by recollecting the shadow: a man recurs to our fancy by remembering his garment, his size or stature, his office or employment, etc. . . .

> *(b)* To this head also we may **refer** that **remembrance of names and things** which may be derived **from our recollection of their likeness to other things** which we know; either their resemblance in name, character, form, accident, or any thing that belongs to them. An idea or word which has been lost or forgotten, has been often recovered by hitting upon some other kindred word or idea which has the nearest resemblance to it, and that in the letters, syllables, or sound of the name, as well as properties of the thing. . . .

> *(c)* And sometimes **a new or strange idea may be fixed in the memory by considering its contrary or opposite.** So if we cannot hit on the word Goliath, the remembrance of David

may recover it; or the name of a Trojan may be recovered by thinking of a Greek, etc.

(8) **In such cases wherein it may be done, seek after a local memory, or a remembrance of what you have read by the side or page of where it is written or printed**; whether the right or the left, whether at the top, the middle, or the bottom; whether at the beginning of a chapter or a paragraph, or the end of it. It has been some advantage, for this reason, to accustom one's self to books of the same edition . . .

(9) **Let every thing we desire to remember be** . . . *legibly* **and distinctly written** and divided into periods, with large characters in the beginning, for by this means we shall the more readily imprint the matter and words on our minds, and recollect them with a glance, the more remarkable the writing appears to the eye. This sense conveys the ideas to the fancy better than any other; and what we have seen is not so soon forgotten as what we have only heard. What Horace affirms of the mind or passions may be said also of memory:

> Sounds which address the ear are lost and die
> In one short hour; but that which strikes the eye
> Lives long upon the mind; the faithful sight
> Engraves the knowledge with a beam of light.

(a) Under this head we may **take notice of the advantage which the memory gains by** having the several objects of our learning drawn out into **schemes and tables**; matters of mathematical science and natural philosophy are not only let into the understanding, but preserved in the memory by figures and diagrams. The situation of the several parts of the earth are better learned by one day's conversing with a map or sea-chart, than by merely reading the description of their situation a hundred times over in books of geography. So the constellations in astronomy, and their position in the heavens, are more easily remembered by hemispheres of the stars well drawn. It is by having such sort of memorials, figures, and tables, hung round our studies or places of residence or resort, that our memory of these things will be greatly assisted and improved, . . .

(b) I might add here also, that **once writing over what we design to remember, and giving due attention to what we write, will fix it more in the mind than reading it five times.** And in the same manner, if we had a plan of the naked lines of longitude and latitude projected on the meridian printed for this use, a learner might much more speedily advance himself in the knowledge of geography by his own drawing the figures of all the parts of the world upon it by imitation, than by many days survey of a map of the world so printed. The same also may be said concerning the constellatons of heaven, drawn by the learner on a naked projection of the circles of the sphere upon the plane of the equator.

(10) **It has sometimes been the practice of men to imprint names or sentences on their memory by taking the first letters of every word of that sentence, or of those names, and making a new word out of them.** ...

But after all, the very writers on this subject have confessed that several of these artificial helps of memory are so cumbersome as not to be suitable to every temper or person; nor are they of any use for the delivery of a discourse by memory, nor of much service in learning the sciences: but they may be sometimes practised for the assisting our remembrance of certain sentences, numbers, and names.

Chapter 12

DETERMINING A QUESTION

In this chapter Dr. Watts addresses how we may determine whether a question should be considered, based upon both its nature and the limitations set by our abilities. If it should be considered, then Dr. Watts advises what steps should be taken to prepare both the question and our attitude for its objective determination.

- Considerations -

(1) When a subject is proposed to your thoughts, **consider whether it be knowable at all**, or no; and then whether it be not above the reach of your inquiry and knowledge in the present state; and remember, that it is *a* great waste of time to busy yourselves too much amongst unsearchables: the chief use of these studies is to keep the mind humble, by finding its own ignorance and weakness.

(2) **Consider** again **whether the matter be worthy of your inquiry** at all; and then how far it may be worthy of your present search and labour according to your age, your time of life, your station in the world, your capacity, your profession, your chief design and end. There are many things worth inquiry to one man, which are not so to another; and there are things that may deserve the study of the same person in one part of life, which would be improper or impertinent at another. ...

(3) **Consider whether** the subject of your inquiry be easy or difficult; whether **you have sufficient foundation or skill**, furniture and advantages **for the pursuit of it**. It would be madness for a young statuary to attempt at first to carve a Venus or a Mercury, and especially without proper tools. And it is equal folly for a man to pretend to make great improvements in natural philosophy without due experiments.

(4) **Consider whether the subject be any ways useful** or no before you engage in the study of it; often put this question to yourselves, ... To what purpose? ... Will the profit be equal to the labour? There are many subtle impertinences learned in the schools; many painful trifles, even among the mathematical theorems and problems; ... or laborious follies of various kinds, which some ingenious men have been engaged in. A due reflection upon these things will call the mind away from vain amusements, and save much time.

(5) **Consider what tendency it has to make you wiser and better,** as well as to make you more learned; and those questions which tend to wisdom and prudence in our conduct among men. ...

- Preparing the Question -

(1) **If** the question appear to be well worth your diligent application, and you are furnished with the necessary requisites to pursue it, then consider whether **it be dressed up and entangled in more words than is needful,** and contain or include more complicated ideas than is necessary; and if so, **endeavour to reduce it to a greater simplicity and plainness,** which will make the inquiry and argument easier and plainer all the way.

If it be stated in an improper, obscure, or irregular form, it may be meliorated by changing the phrase, or transposing the parts of it; but be careful always to keep the grand and important point of inquiry the same in your new stating *of* the question. Little tricks and deceits of sophistry, by sliding in or leaving out such words as entirely change the question, should be abandoned and renounced by all fair disputants and honest searchers after truth.

(2) **The stating a question with clearness** and justice **goes a great way,** many times, **toward the answering *of* it.** The greatest part of true knowledge lies in a distinct perception of things which are in themselves distinct; and some men give more light and knowledge by the bare stating of the question with perspicuity and justice, than others by talking of it in gross confusion for whole hours together. To state a question is but to separate and disentangle the parts of it from one another, as well as from every thing which does not concern the question, and then lay the disentangled parts of the question in due order and method: oftentimes, without more ado,

this fully resolves the doubt, and shews the mind where the truth lies, without argument or dispute.

(3) **If the question relate to an axiom**, or first principle of truth, remember that a long train of consequences may depend upon it; therefore **it should not be suddenly admitted or received.**

    (a) **It is not enough** to determine the truth of a proposition, much less to raise it to the honour of an axiom or first principle, **to say that it has been believed through many ages,** that it has been received by many nations, that it is almost universally acknowledged, or nobody denies it, that it is established by human laws or that temporal penalties or reproaches will attend the disbelief of it.

    (b) **Nor is it enough to forbid any proposition the title of axiom, because it has been denied** by some persons, and doubted of by others; for some persons have been unreasonably credulous, and others have been as unreasonably skeptical. Then only should a proposition be called an axiom, or a self-evident truth, when, by a moderate attention to the subject and predicate, their connection appears in so plain a light, and so clear an evidence, as needs no third idea, or middle term, to prove them to be connected.

(4) **While** you are **in search after truth** in questions of a doubtful nature, or such as you have not yet thoroughly examined, **keep up a just indifference to either side of the question,** if you would be led honestly into the truth: for a desire or inclination leaning to either side biasses the judgment strangely: whereas by this indifference for everything but truth, you will be excited to examine fairly instead of presuming, and your assent will be secured from going beyond your evidence.

    (a) For the most part people are born to their opinions, and never question the truth of what their family, or their country, or their party profess. They clothe their minds as they do their bodies, after the fashion in vogue, nor one of a hundred ever examine their principles. It is suspected of lukewarmness, to suppose examination necessary; and it will be charged as a tendency to apostasy, if we go about to examine them. Persons are applauded for presuming they are in the right, and (as Mr.

Locke saith) he that considers and inquires into the reason of things is counted a foe to orthodoxy, because possibly he may deviate from some of the received doctrines. And thus **men without any industry or acquisition of their own** (lazy and idle as they are) **inherit local truths,** i.e. the truths of that place where they live, and are inured to assent without evidence.

(b) This hath a long and unhappy influence; for **if a man can bring his mind once to be positive and fierce for propositions whose evidence he hath never examined,** and that in matters of the greatest concernment, **he will** naturally follow this short and easy way of judging and believing in cases of less moment, and **build all his opinions upon insufficient grounds.**

- Determining the Question -

(1) In determining a question, especially when it is a matter of difficulty and importance, **do not take up with partial examination, but turn your thoughts on all sides**, to gather in all the light you can toward the solution of it. Take time, and use all the helps that are to be attained, before you fully determine, except only where present necessity of action calls for speedy determination.

If you would know what may be called a partial examination, take these instances, viz. . . .

If it be a question which is to be determined by reason and argument, then your examination is partial when you turn the question only in one light, and do not turn it on all sides: when you look upon it only in its relations and aspects to one sort of object, and not to another; when you consider only the advantages of it, and the reasons for it, and neglect to think of the reasons against it, and never survey its inconveniences too; when you determine on a sudden, before you have given yourself a due time for weighing all circumstances, etc.

Again, if it be a question of fact, depending upon the report or testimony of men, your examination is but partial when you inquire only what one man or a few say, and avoid the testimony of others; when you only ask what those report who were not eye or ear witnesses, and neglect those who saw and heard it; when you content yourself with mere loose and general talk about it, and never enter into particulars; or when there are many who deny the fact, and you never concern yourself about their reasons for denying it, but resolve to believe only those who affirm it. ...

... These are all instances of imperfect examination: and we should never determine a question by one or two lights, where we may have the advantage of three or four.

(2) **Take heed lest some darling notion**, some favourite hypothesis, some beloved doctrine, or some common but unexamined opinion, **be made a test of the truth or falsehood of all other propositions about the same subject.** Dare not build much upon such a notion or doctrine till it be very fully examined, accurately adjusted, and sufficiently confirmed. ...

(3) For the same reason, **have a care of suddenly determining any one question on which the determination of any kindred or parallel cases will** easily or naturally **follow.** Take heed of receiving any wrong turn in your early judgment of things; be watchful as far as possible against any false bias which may be given to the understanding, especially in younger years. The indulgence of some one silly opinion, or the giving credit to one foolish fable, lays the mind open to be imposed upon by many. The ancient Romans were taught to believe that Romulus and Remus, the founders of their state and empire, were exposed in the woods, and nursed by a wolf: this story prepared their minds for the reception of any tales of the like nature relating to other countries. ...

So the child who is once taught to believe any one occurrence to be a good or evil omen, or any day of the month or week to be lucky or unlucky, hath a wide inroad made on the soundness of his understanding in the following judgments of his life; he lies ever open to all the silly impressions and idle tales of nurses, and imbibes many a foolish story with greediness, which he must unlearn again if ever he become acquainted with truth and wisdom. ...

(4) As a warm zeal ought never to be employed in the defence of any revealed truth, till our reason be well convinced of the revelation; so neither should wit and banter, jest and ridicule, ever be indulged to oppose or assault any doctrines of professed revelation, till reason has proved they are not really revealed; and even then these methods should be used very seldom, and with the utmost caution and prudence. **Raillery and wit were never made to answer our**

inquiries after truth, and to determine a question of rational controversy; though they may sometimes be serviceable to expose to contempt those inconsistent follies which have been first abundantly refuted by argument; they serve indeed only to cover nonsense with shame, when reason has first proved it to be mere nonsense. ...

(5) In reading philosophical, moral, or religious controversies, never raise your esteem of any opinion by the assurance and zeal wherewith the author asserts it, nor by the highest praises he bestows upon it; nor, on the other hand, let your esteem of an opinion be abated, nor your aversion to it raised by the supercilious contempt cast upon it by a warm writer, nor by the sovereign airs with which he condemns it. **Let the force of argument alone influence your assent or dissent**. Take care that your soul be not warped or biassed on one side or the other by any strains of flattering or abusive language; for there is no question whatsoever but what hath some such sort of defenders and opposers. Leave those writers to their own follies who practise thus upon the weakness of their readers without argument; leave them to triumph in their own fancied possessions and victories: it is oftentimes found that their possessions are but a heap of errors, and their boasted victories are but overbearing noise and clamour to silence the voice of truth.

In philosophy and religion the bigots of all parties are generally the most positive, and deal much in this sort of argument. Sometimes these are the weapons of pride, for a haughty man supposes all his opinions to be infallible, and imagines the contrary sentiments are ever ridiculous and not worthy of notice. Sometimes these ways of talking are the mere arms of ignorance: the men who use them know little of the opposite side of the question, and therefore they exult in their own vain pretences to knowledge, as though no man of sense could oppose their opinions. They rail at an objection against their own sentiments, because they can find no other answer to it but railing. And men of learning, by their excessive vanity, have been sometimes tempted into the same insolent practice as well as the ignorant.

Yet let it be remembered too, that there are some truths so plain and evident, that the opposition to them is strange, unaccountable, and almost monstrous: and in vindication of such truths a writer of good sense may sometimes be allowed to use a degree of assurance, and pronounce them strongly with an air of confidence, while he defends them with reasons of convincing force.

(6) **Sometimes a question** may be proposed which **is of so large and extensive** a nature, and refers to such a multitude of subjects, **as ought not** in justice **to be determined** at once **by a single argument or answer**: as if one should ask me, Are you a professed disciple of the Stoics or the Platonists? Do you receive an assent to the principles of Gassendus, Descartes, or Sir Isaac Newton? Have you chosen the hypothesis of Tycho or Copernicus? . . . I think it may be very proper in such cases not to give an answer in the gross, but rather to enter into a detail of particulars, and explain one's own sentiments. Perhaps there is no man, nor set of men upon earth, whose sentiments I entirely follow. . . . Though I may see sufficient ground to agree to the greatest part of the opinions of one person or party, yet it does by no means follow that I should receive them all. Truth does not always go by the lump, nor does error tincture and spoil all the articles of belief that some one party professes. . . .

(7) When you are called in the course of life or religion to judge and determine concerning any question, and to affirm or deny it, **take a full survey of the objections against it, as well as of the arguments for it**, as far as your time and circumstances admit, **and see on which side the preponderation falls**. If either the objections against any proposition, or the arguments for the defence of it, carry in them most undoubted evidence, and are plainly unanswerable, they will and ought to constrain the assent, though there may be many seeming probabilities on the other side, which at first sight would flatter the judgment to favour it. But where the reasons on both sides are very near of equal weight, there suspension or doubt is our duty, unless in cases wherein present determination or practice is required, and there we must act according to the present appearing preponderation of reasons.

(8) **In matters of moment and importance, it is our duty indeed to seek after certain and conclusive arguments** (if they can be found) in order to determine a question; but where the matter is of little consequence, it is not worth our labour to spend much time in seeking after certainties; it is sufficient here, if probable reasons

offer themselves. And even in matters of greater importance, especially where daily practice is necessary, and where we cannot attain any sufficient or certain grounds to determine a question on either side, we must then take up with such probable arguments as we can arrive at. But this general rule should be observed, viz. to take heed that our assent be no stronger, or rise no higher in the degree of it, than the probable argument will support.

(9) There are **many things** even in religion, as well as in philosophy and civil life, **which we believe with very different degrees of assent**; and this is, or **should be**, always **regulated according to the different degrees of evidence** which we enjoy: and perhaps there are a thousand gradations in our assent to the things we believe, because there are thousands of circumstances relating to different questions, which increase or diminish the evidence we have concerning them, and that in matters both of reason and revelation. ...

- Judging of Probabilities -

We may observe ... *the following* three rules in judging of probabilities which are to be determined by reason, relating either to things past or things to come.

(1) **That which agrees most with the constitution of nature carries the greatest probability in it,** where no other circumstance appears to counterpoise it: as if I let loose a greyhound within sight of a hare upon a large plain, there is great probability the greyhound will seize her; that a thousand sparrows will fly away at the sight of a hawk among them.

(2) **That which is most conformable to the constant observations of men**, or to experiments frequently repeated, **is most likely to be true**: as that a winter will not pass away in England without some frost and snow; that if you deal out great quantities of strong liquor to the mob, there will be many drunk; that a large assembly of men will be of different opinions in any doubtful point; that a thief will make his escape out of prison if the doors of it are unguarded at midnight.

(3) In matters of fact, which are past or present, **where neither nature, nor observation, nor custom gives us any sufficient information** on either side of the question, there **we may derive a probability from the attestation of wise and honest men,** by word or writing, or the

concurring witnesses of multitudes who have seen and known what they relate, etc. This testimony in many cases will arise to the degree of moral certainty. So we believe that the plant tea grows in China; and that the emperor of the Turks lives at Constantinople. ...

- Conclusion -

When a point hath been well examined, and our own judgment settled upon just arguments in our manly age, and after a large survey of the merits of the cause, it would be a weakness for us always to continue fluttering in suspense. We ought therefore to stand firm in such well-established principles, and not be tempted to change and alter for the sake of every difficulty, or every occasional objection. We are not to be carried about with every flying doctrine, like children tossed to and fro and wavering with the wind. ...

In short, those truths which are the springs of daily practice should be settled as soon as we can with the exercise of our best powers after the state of manhood: but those things wherein we may possibly mistake should never be so absolutely and finally established and determined as though we were infallible. ...

Appendix A

A GUARD AGAINST EVIL INFLUENCES
FROM PERSONS AND THINGS

It belongs also to a good education that children be guarded and secured, as far as possible, from all evil influences and unhappy impressions which they may be exposed to receive both from persons and things. I shall sufficiently explain this direction by particular instances.

Let not nurses or servants be suffered to fill their minds with silly tales and with senseless rhymes, many of which are so absurd and ridiculous, that they will not bear to be represented in a grave discourse. The imagination of young creatures is hereby flattered and deceived: their reason is grossly abused and imposed upon: and by this means they are trained up to be amused with follies and nonsense, rather than to exercise their understanding, which is the glory of human nature.

Let not any persons that are near them terrify their tender minds with dismal stories of witches and ghosts, of devils and evil spirits, of fairies and bugbears in the dark. This hath had a most mischievous effect on some children, and hath fixed in their constitutions such a rooted slavery and fear, that they have scarce dared to be left alone all their lives, especially in the night. These stories have made such a deep and frightful impression on their tender fancies, that it hath enervated their souls, it hath grown up with them, and, mingled with their religion, it hath laid a wretched foundation for melancholy and distracting sorrows. Let these sort of informations be reserved for their firmer years, and let them not be told in their hearing till they can better judge what truth or reality there is in them, and be made sensible how much is owing to romance and fiction.

Nor let their little hearts be frightened at three or four years old with shocking and bloody histories, with massacres and martyrdoms, with cuttings and burnings, with the images of horrible and barbarous murders, with racks and red-hot pincers, with engines of torment and cruelty, with mangled limbs, and carcases drenched in gore. It is time enough, when their spirits are grown a little firmer, to acquaint them with these madnesses and miseries of human nature. There is no need that the history of the holy confessors and martyrs should be set before their thoughts so early, in all their most ghastly shapes and colours. These things, when they are a little older, may be of excellent use to discover to them the wicked and bloody principles of persecution ...

Let their ears be ever kept from all immodest stories and from wanton songs; from riddles and puns with double meanings and foul intentions: let them not be suffered to read wanton jests or amorous romances: and due care should be taken to remove all books out of their way that may defile their imagination, or teach them the language or the sentiments of impurity. Nor let their eyes be entertained with lewd and unclean pictures, and images of things or actions that are not fit to be exposed. These things indeed have too often an unhappy influence to corrupt the fancy and manners; and in riper years have been the occasion of numberless mischiefs: but especially they should be kept far away from the sight or hearing of children, lest too deep and dangerous impressions be made in those early years of life. Nothing but what is chaste, pure, and innocent, should come within the reach of their eyes and ears. Even the common necessities and actions of nature should be always expressed before them in the most modest forms of speech that our mother tongue can furnish us with. In this respect, as the poet says, children should be treated with great reverence. ...

It is confessed that the books of anatomy, and other parts of necessary science, are proper to be written, and these may be consulted by persons who are grown up to a due age, especially by those whose profession requires it: there is also some necessity of foul narratives, where foul crimes are committed, and ought to be publicly exposed and brought to justice and punishment. As the affairs of mankind stand, these things cannot always be avoided; but there is no manner of necessity that children should read them, ...

Let parents take as much care as they can in the choice of companions and play-fellows for their sons and daughters. It would be a happy thing if children who are bred up in schools, could be secured from the company and evil influence of other children, who curse and swear, ... and use filthy and unclean language. Masters and mistresses should be very watchful and strict in their inquiries into the behavior of their scholars of both sexes when they are out of their sight, that, if it were possible, there might not be one among them whose lips are impure or profane: for one diseased sheep may infect the whole flock. However, where children find such immoralities practised by any of their fellows, they should be taught to shew their utmost abhorrence of it, and speedily forsake such pernicious company.

Appendix B

SOCRATIC, FORENSIC, AND ACADEMIC METHODS OF DISPUTATION

The material presented in this appendix regarding formal methods of disputation (Socratic, forensic, and academic or scholastic) was extracted from Dr. Watts' book, Improvement of the Mind. *Elements of the Socratic method are present in the dialogue between teacher and student, lawyer and hostile witness, characters in some books to establish a point of view or a philosophical truth, etc. The forensic method is the basis of dispute and debate in courts of law, the congresses and senates of state and federal governments, town meetings, etc. The academic method is used by debating societies, candidates for public office during debates, etc. Thus, there is merit in a person becoming familiar with these three methods, whether he be an observer or a participant.*

B.1 The Socratical Way of Disputation

This method of dispute derives its name from Socrates, by whom it was practised, and by other philosophers in his age, ...

The Socratical way is managed by questions and answers ...

Now the advantages of this method are very considerable.

(1) It represents a form of a dialogue or common conversation, which is a much more easy, more pleasant, and more sprightly way of instruction, and more fit to excite the attention, and sharpen the penetration of the learner, than solitary reading or silent attention to a lecture. Man being a sociable creature, delights more in conversation, and learns better this way, if it could always be wisely and happily practised.

(2) This method hath something very obliging in it, and carries a very humble and condescending air, when he that instructs seems to be the inquirer, and seeks information from him who learns.

(3) It leads the learner into the knowledge of truth as it were by his own invention, which is a very pleasing thing to human nature; and by questions pertinently and artificially proposed, it does as effectually draw him on to discover his own mistakes, which he is much more easily persuaded to relinquish when he seems to have discovered them himself.

(4) It is managed in a great measure in the form of the most easy reasoning, always arising from something asserted or known in the foregoing answer, and so proceeding to inquire something unknown in the following question, which again makes way for the next answer. Now such an exercise is very alluring and entertaining to the understanding, while its own reasoning powers are all along employed, and that without labour or difficulty, because the querist finds out and proposes all the intermediate ideas or middle terms.

B.2 Forensic Disputes

The forum was a public place in Rome where the lawyers and orators made their speeches before the proper judge in matters of property, or in criminal cases, to accuse or excuse, to complain or defend; thence all sorts of disputations in public assemblies or courts of justice, where several persons make their distinct speeches for or against any person or thing whatsoever, but more especially in civic matters, may come under the name of Forensic disputes.

This is practised not only in the courts of judicature, where a single person sits to judge of the truth or goodness of any cause, and to determine according to the weight of reasons on either side; but it is used also in political senates or parliaments, ecclesiastical synods and assemblies of various kinds.

In these assemblies, generally one person is chosen chairman or moderator, not to give a determination to the controversy, but chiefly to keep the several speakers to the rules of order and decency in their conduct; but the final determination of the question arises from the majority of opinions or votes in the assembly, according as they are or ought to be swayed by the superior weight of reason appearing in the several speeches that are made.

The method of proceeding is usually in some such form as this.

(1) The first person who speaks when the court is set, opens the case either more briefly or at large, and proposes the case to the judge or the chairman, or moderator of the assembly, and gives his own reasons for his opinion in the case proposed.

(2) This person is succeeded by one, or perhaps two, or several more, who paraphrase on the same subject, and argue on the same side of the question: they confirm what the first has spoken, and urge new reasons to enforce the same: then those who are of a different opinion stand up and make their several speeches in a succession, opposing the cause which others have maintained, giving their reasons against it, and endeavouring to refute the arguments whereby the first speakers have supported it.

(3) After this, one and another rises up to make their replies, to vindicate or to condemn, to establish or to confute what has been offered before on each side of the question;

(4) Till at last, according to the rules, orders, or customs of the court or assembly, the controversy is decided, either by a single judge, or the suffrage of the assembly.

Where the question or matter in debate consists of several parts, after it is once opened by the first or second speaker, sometimes those who follow take each of them a particular part of the debate, according to their inclination or their prior agreement, and apply themselves to argue upon that single point only, that so the whole complexion of the debate may not be thrown into confusion by the variety of subjects, if every speaker should handle all the subjects of debate.

Before the final sentence of determination is given, it is usual to have the reasons and arguments, which have been offered on both sides, summed up and represented in a more compendious manner; and this is done either by the appointed judge of the court, or the chairman, or some noted person in the assembly, that so judgment may proceed upon the fullest survey of the whole subject, that as far as possible in human affairs nothing may be done contrary to truth or justice.

As this is a practice in which multitudes of gentlemen, besides those of the learned professions, may be engaged, at least, in their maturer years of life, so it would be a very proper and useful thing to introduce this custom into our academies, viz. to propose cases, and let the students debate them in a forensic manner in the presence of their tutors. There was something of this kind practised by the Roman youth in their schools, in order to train them up for orators, both in the forum and in the senate. . . .

B.3 Academic or Scholastic Disputation

The common methods in which disputes are managed in the schools of learning are these, viz.

(1) The tutor appoints a question in some of the sciences, to be debated amongst his students: one of them undertakes to affirm or to deny the question, and to defend his assertion or negation, and to answer all objections against it; he is called the respondent: and the rest of the students in the same class, or who pursue the same science, are the opponents, who are appointed to dispute or raise objections against the proposition thus affirmed or denied.

(2) Each of the students successively in their turn becomes the respondent or the defender of that proposition, while the rest oppose it also successively in their turns.

(3) It is the business of the respondent to write a . . . short discourse on the question proposed; and he either affirms or denies the question, according to the opinion of the tutor, which is supposed to be the truth, and he reads it at the beginning of the dispute.

(4) In his discourse (which is written with as great accuracy as the youth is capable of) he explains the terms of the question, frees them from all ambiguity, fixes their sense, declares the true intent and meaning of the question itself, separates it from other questions with which it may have been complicated, and distinguishes it from other questions which may happen to be akin to it, and then pronounces in the negative or affirmative concerning it.

(5) When this is done, then, in the second part of his discourse, he gives his own strongest arguments to confirm the proposition he has laid down, i.e., to vindicate his own side of the question; but he does not usually proceed to represent the objections against it, and to solve or answer them; for it is the business of the other students to raise objections in disputing. . . .

During this time the tutor sits in the chair as president or moderator, to see that the rules of disputation and decency be observed on both sides; and to admonish each disputant of any irregularity in their conduct. His work is also to illustrate and explain the answer or distinction of the respondent where it is obscure, to strengthen it where it is weak, and to correct it where it is false: and when the respondent is pinched with a strong objection, and is at a loss for an answer, the moderator assists him, and suggests some answer to the question, according to his own opinion or sentiment.

In public disputes, where the opponents and repondents choose their own side of the question, the moderator's work is not to favour either disputant; but he only sits as president, to see that the laws of disputation be observed, and a decorum maintained.

Now the laws of disputation relate either to the opponent or to the respondent, or to both.

The laws obliging the opponent are these:

(1) That he must directly contradict the proposition of the respondent, and not merely attack any of the arguments whereby the respondent has supported that proposition; for it is one thing to refute a single argument of the respondent, and another to confute the thesis itself.

(2) ... He must contradict or oppose the very sense and intention of the proposition as the respondent has stated it, and not merely oppose the words of the thesis in any other sense: for this would be the way to plunge the dispute into ambiguity and darkness, to talk beside the question, to wrangle about the words, and to attack a proposition different from what the respondent has espoused, ...

(3) He must propose his argumenta in a plain, short, and syllogistic form, according to the rules of logic, without flying to fallacies or sophisms, and as far as may be, he should use categorical syllogisms.

(4) Though the respondent may be attacked either upon a point of his own concession, which is called argumentum ex concessis, or by reducing him to an absurdity, which is called reductio ad absurdum, yet it is the neatest, the most useful, and the best sort of disputation, where the opponent draws his objections from the nature of the question itself.

(5) Where the respondent denies any proposition, the opponent, if he proceed, must directly vindicate and confirm that proposition, i.e. he must make that proposition the conclusion of his next syllogism.

(6) Where the respondent limits or distinguishes any proposition, the opponent must directly prove his own proposition in that sense, and according to that member of the distinction in which the respondent denied it.

The laws that oblige the respondent are these:

(1) To repeat the argument of the opponent in the very same words in which it was proposed, before he attempts to answer it.

(2) If the syllogism be false in the logical form of it, he must discover the fault according to the rules of logic.

(3) If the argument does not directly and effectually oppose his thesis, he must shew this mistake, and make it appear that his thesis is safe, even though the argument of the opponent be admitted; or, at least, that the argument does only aim at it collaterally, or at a distance, and not directly overthrow it, or conclude against it.

(4) Whether the matter of the opponent's objection is faulty in any part of it, the respondent must grant what is true in it, he must deny what is false, he must distinguish or limit the proposition which is ambiguous or doubtful, and then, granting the sense in which it is true, he must deny the sense in which it is false.

(5) If an hypothetic proposition be false, the respondent must deny the consequence; if a disjunctive, he must deny the disjunction; if a categoric or relative, he must simply deny it.

(6) It is sometimes allowed for the respondent to use an indirect answer after he has answered directly; and he may also shew how the opponent's argument may be retorted against himself.

The laws that oblige both disputants are these:

(1) Sometimes it is necessary there should be a mention of certain general principles in which they both agree, relating to the question, that so they may not dispute on those things which either are or ought to have been first granted on both sides.

(2) When the state of the controversy is well known, and plainly determined and agreed, it must not be altered by either disputant

in the course of the disputation; and the respondent especially should keep a watchful eye on the opponent in this matter.

(3) Let neither party invade the province of the other; especially let the respondent take heed that he does not turn opponent, except in retorting the argument upon his adversary after a direct response; and even this is allowed only as an illustration or confirmation of his own response.

(4) Let each wait with patience till the other has done speaking. It is a piece of rudeness to interrupt another in his speech.

Yet, though the disputants have not this liberty, the moderator may do it, when either of the disputants break the rules, and he may interpose so far as to keep them in order.

It must be confessed there are some advantages to be attained by academical disputation. It gives vigour and briskness to the mind thus exercised, and relieves the langour of private study and meditation. It sharpens the wit, and all the inventive powers. It makes thoughts active, and sends them on all sides to find arguments and answers both for opposition and defence. It gives opportunity of viewing the subject of discourse on all sides, and of learning what inconveniences, difficulties, and objections, attend particular opinions. It furnishes the soul with various occasions of starting such thoughts as otherwise would never have come into the mind. It makes a student more expert in attacking and refuting an error, as well as in vindicating a truth. It instructs the scholar in the various methods of warding off the force of objections, and of discovering and repelling the subtle tricks of sophisters. It procures also a freedom and readiness of speech, and raises the modest and diffident genius to a due degree of courage.

But there are some very grievous inconveniences that may sometimes overbalance all these advantages. For many young students, by a constant habit of disputing, grow impudent and audacious, proud and disdainful, talkative and impertinent, and render themselves intolerable by an obstinate humour of maintaining whatever they have asserted, as well as by a spirit of contradiction, opposing almost every thing that they hear. The disputation itself often awakens the passions of ambition, emulation, and anger; it carries away the mind from that calm and sedate temper which is so necessary to contemplate truth.

It is evident also, that by frequent exercises of this sort, wherein opinions true and false are argued, supported, and refuted on both sides, the mind of man is led by insensible degrees to an uncertainty and fluctuating temper, and falls into danger of a sceptical humour, which never comes to an establishment in any doctrines. Many persons, by this means, become much more ready to oppose whatsoever is offered in searching out truth; they hardly wait till they have read or heard the sentiment of any person, before their heads are busily employed to seek out arguments against it. They grow naturally sharp in finding out difficulties; and by indulging this humour, they converse with the dark and doubtful parts of a subject so long, till they almost render themselves incapable of receiving the full evidence of a proposition, and acknowledging the light of truth. It has some tendency to make a youth a carping critic, rather than a judicious man. ...

General directions for scholastic disputes:

(1) Never dispute upon mere trifles, things that are utterly useless to be known, ...

(2) Do not make infinite and unsearchable things the matter of dispute, nor such propositions as are made up of mere words without ideas, ...

(3) Let not obvious and known truths, or some of the most plain and certain propositions, be bandied about in a disputation, for a mere trial of skill; for he that opposes them in this manner, will be in danger of contracting a habit of opposing all evidence, ...

(4) It would be well if every dispute could be so ordered as to be a means of searching out truth, and not to gain a triumph. ...

For this end, let both the respondent and opponent use the clearest and most distinct and expressive language in which they can clothe their thoughts. Let them seek and practise brevity and perspicuity on both sides, without long declamations, tedious circumlocutions, and rhetorical flourishes. ...

(5) They should not indulge ridicule, either of persons or things, in their disputations. They should abstain from all banter and jest, laughter and merriment. ... However an argument on some subjects may be sometimes clothed with a little pleasantry, ...

(6) Nor should sarcasm and reproach, or insolent language, ever be used among fair disputants. Turn not off from things to speak of persons. ...

(7) If the opponent sees victory to incline to his side, let him be content to shew the force of his argument to the intelligent part of the company, without too importunate and petulant demands of an answer, and without insulting over his antagonist, or putting the modesty of the respondent to the blush. Nor let the respondent triumph over the opponent when he is silent and replies no more. ...

(8) Might it not be a safer practice, in order to attain the best ends of disputation, and to avoid some of the ill effects of it, if the opponents were sometimes engaged on the side of truth, and produced their arguments in opposition to error? And what if the respondent was appointed to support the error, and defend it as well as he could, till he was forced to yield at least to those arguments of the opponent which appear to be really just, and strong, and unanswerable? ...

Upon the whole, it seems necessary that these methods of disputation should be learned in the schools, in order to teach students better to defend truth, and to refute error, both in writing and conversation, where the scholastic forms are utterly neglected.

But after all, the advantage which youth may gain by disputations depends much on the tutor or moderator; he should manage with such prudence, both in the disputation and at the end of it, as to make all the disputants know the very point of controversy wherein it consists; he should manifest the fallacy of sophistical objections, and confirm the solid arguments and answers. This might teach students how to make the art of disputation useful for the searching out the truth and the defence of it, that it may not be learned and practised only as an art of wrangling, ...

Appendix C

SYNOPSIS OF THE CHAPTERS

As stated in the preface, the major theme in each numbered section of each chapter is denoted by the use of **bold** *type. These themes have been extracted and compiled in this appendix to provide:*

- *A quick reference to the contents and essence of each chapter.*
- *A study guide.*
- *A vehicle to refresh the memory.*

Because the major themes may occasionally be found ambiguous when taken out of context, the editors, when necessary, have provided additional words or expressions (indicated by italic type) to clarify meanings.

Chapter 1: GENERAL RULES FOR THE IMPROVEMENT OF KNOWLEDGE

- Rules

  (1) Deeply possess your mind with the vast importance of a good judgment, and the rich and inestimable advantage of right reasoning.

  (2) Consider the weaknesses, frailties, and mistakes of human nature in general, which arise from the very constitution of a soul united to an animal body.

  (3) Contrive and practice some proper methods to acquaint yourself with your own ignorance.

    (a) Take a wide survey now and then of the vast and unlimited regions of learning.

(b) Think what a numberless variety of questions and difficulties there are belonging even to that particular science in which you have made the greatest progress.

(c) Spend a few thoughts sometimes on puzzling inquiries to give you a more sensible impression of the poverty of your understanding and the imperfection of your knowledge.

(d) Read the accounts of those vast treasures of knowledge which some of the dead have possessed, and some of the living do possess.

(4) Presume not too much upon a bright genius, a ready wit, and good parts; for this, without labour and study, will never make a man of knowledge and wisdom.

(5) As you are not to fancy yourself a learned man because you are blessed with a ready wit; so neither must you imagine that large and laborious reading, and a strong memory, can denominate you truly wise.

(6) Be not so weak as to imagine that a life of learning is a life of laziness and ease.

(7) Let the hope of new discoveries, as well as the satisfaction and pleasure of known truths, animate your daily industry.

(8) Do not hover always on the surface of things.

(9) Once a day, especially in the early years of life and study, call yourselves to an account what new ideas, what new proposition or truth you have gained, what further confirmation of known truths, and what advances you have made in any part of knowledge.

(10) Maintain a constant watch at all times against a dogmatical spirit.

(a) It stops the ear against all further reasoning upon that subject, and shuts up the mind from all further improvements of knowledge.

(b) A dogmatical spirit naturally leads us to arrogance of mind, and gives a man some airs in conversation which are too haughty and assuming.

(11) Though caution and slow assent will guard you against frequent mistakes and retractions; yet you should get humility and courage enough to retract any mistake, and confess an error.

(12) He that would raise his judgment above the vulgar rank of mankind, and learn to pass a just sentence on persons and things, must take heed of a fanciful temper of mind, and a humorous conduct in his affairs.

(13) Have a care of trifling with things important and momentous, or to sporting with things awful and sacred: do not indulge a spirit of ridicule.

(14) Ever maintain a virtuous and pious frame of spirit.

(15) Watch against the pride of your own reason, and a vain conceit of your own intellectual powers.

Chapter 2: OBSERVATION, READING, INSTRUCTION BY LECTURES, CONVERSATION, AND STUDY, COMPARED

- General Definitions

    (1) Observation is the notice that we take of all occurrences.

    (2) Reading is that means or method of knowledge whereby we acquaint ourselves with what other men have written.

    (3) Public or private lectures are such verbal instructions as are given by a teacher.

    (4) Conversation is another method of improving our minds, wherein, by mutual discourse and inquiry, we learn the sentiments of others.

    (5) Meditation or study includes all those exercises of the mind, whereby we render all the former methods useful.

- Advantages of each method

    (1) Observation

    (a) *Furnishes* first simple and complex ideas.

    (b) Knowledge gotten at first hand.

    (c) Gain knowledge all the day long.

    (2) Reading

(a) We acquaint ourselves with the affairs, actions, and thoughts of the living and the dead.

(b) We transfer to ourselves products of great and wise men in their several ages and nations.

(c) We learn the best, the most laboured, and most refined sentiments.

(d) We may review what we have read.

(3) Lectures

(a) *Lectures are* more delightful and entertaining than reading.

(b) A tutor or instructor, when he paraphrases and explains other authors can mark out the precise point of difficulty or controversy.

(c) *Lectures* can convey to our senses those notions which cannot so well be done by mere reading.

(d) *We* have *the* opportunity to inquire how a difficulty may be explained and removed.

(4) Conversation

(a) When we converse familiarly with a learned friend we have his own help at hand to explain to us.

(b) We may propose our doubts and objections and have them solved and answered at once.

(c) Difficulties we meet with in books, and in our private studies, may find a relief by friendly conference.

(d) *Conversation* calls out into light what has been lodged in all the recesses and secret chambers of the soul.

(e) *Our* intellectual powers are more animated.

(f) We have a great advantage of proposing our private opinions and bringing our own sentiments to the test.

(g) Conversation furnishes *us* with the knowledge of men and the affairs of life.

(5) Meditation or study

(a) Our own meditation and the labour of our own thoughts form our judgment of things.

(b) Meditation transfers and conveys the notions and sentiments of others to ourselves.

(c) We improve the hints that we have acquired by observation, conversation, lecture, and reading.

Chapter 3: RULES RELATING TO OBSERVATION

- Rules

    (1) Let the enlargement of knowledge be one constant view and design in life.

    (2) The laudable curiosity of young people should be indulged and gratified, rather than discouraged.

    (3) Write down what is most remarkable and uncommon.

    (4) Keep our minds as free as possible from passions and prejudices.

    (5) Beware of indulging that busy curiosity which is ever inquiring into private and domestic affairs.

    (6) Let your observation be chiefly designed to lead you to a better acquaintance with things.

    (7) Remarks you make on particular persons, especially to their disadvantage, should for the most part lie hid in your own breast.

    (8) Be not too hasty to erect general theories from a few particular observations, appearances, or experiments.

Chapter 4: BOOKS AND READING

- Selecting Books

    (1) It is of vast advantage to have the most proper books for reading recommended by a judicious friend.

- Books of Importance

    (1) Books of importance of any kind should be first read in a more general and cursory manner.

    (2) If three or four persons agree to read the same book, *it* will render the reading beneficial to every one of them.

    (3) Several persons engaged in the same study promote each other's improvement.

    (4) Your chief business is to consider whether *the authors'* opinions are right or no, and to improve your own solid knowledge.

(5) If a writer does not explain his ideas or prove the positions well, mark the faults or defects and endeavour to do it better.

(6) If the method of a book be irregular, reduce it into form by a little analysis of your own.

(7) If a book has no index to it, or good table of contents, make one.

(8) Make all your reading subservient not only to the enlargement of your treasures of knowledge, but also to the improvement of your reasoning powers.

(9) Be diligent into the sense and arguments of the authors.

(10) Never apply yourselves to read any author with a determination beforehand either for or against him.

> *(a)* Nor should any of our opinions be so resolved upon, especially in younger years, as never to hear or to bear opposition to them.

> *(b)* When we peruse those authors who defend our own settled sentiments, we should not take all their arguments for just and solid.

> *(c)* When we read those authors which oppose our most certain and established principles, we should be ready to receive any informations from them in other points.

(11) When our consciences are convinced that these rules of prudence or duty belong to us, and require our conformity to them, we should then call ourselves to account.

- Books of Diversion and Amusement

  (1) All those paragraphs or sentiments deserve a remark, which are new and uncommon, noble and excellent, strong and convincing, beautiful and elegant, or any way worthy.

  (2) Writings as may happen to be remarkably stupid or silly, false or mistaken, should become subjects of an occasional criticism.

  (3) Where the poesy, oratory, etc. shine, a single reading is not sufficient.

- Books that Sharpen our Literary Comprehension

  (1) Vocabularies and dictionaries are to be consulted, and never let an unknown word pass in your reading without seeking for its sense and meaning.

- Scholar vs. Mere Collector

  (1) Be not satisfied with a mere knowledge of the best authors that treat of any subject. *Otherwise, you are under a great temptation to practise the following two follies:*

    (a) Furnish *your* library infinitely better than *your* understanding.

    (b) At best *your* learning reaches no further than the indexes and table of contents.

Chapter 5: JUDGMENT OF BOOKS

(1) *If we would* form a judgment of a book which we have not seen before, the title-page, the author's name, the preface, *and the table of contents* may assist our judgment.

(2) *Run through several chapters to* judge whether the treatise be worth a complete perusal or no.

(3) General mistakes.

  (a) We are ready to pass a favourable judgment if *a book* agrees with our own principles.

  (b) *We may* admire *a* treatise whereas if *we* had but attained a good degree of skill in that science, perhaps *we* would find that the author had written very poorly.

  (c) When we have made ourselves masters of any particular theme of knowledge, we knew most of those things before, and therefore they strike us not, and we are in danger of discommending them.

(4) More of these follies.

  (a) There are some persons who will give their judgment on a book as soon as the title of it is mentioned, though they have neither studied nor understood it.

  (b) Another sort of judges become mere echoes of the praises or censures of other men.

(5) It is a paltry humour that inclines a man to rail at any human performance because it is not absolutely perfect.

(6) Another very frequent fault is this, that persons spread the same praises or the same reproaches over a whole treatise, and all the chapters in it, which are due only to some of them.

(7) When you hear any person pretending to give his judgment of a book, consider whether he be a capable judge.

Chapter 6: LIVING INSTRUCTIONS AND LECTURES; TEACHERS AND LEARNERS

• Introduction

(1) Assistance of teachers is absolutely necessary for most persons.

• Selection of Instructors

(1) It is best to enjoy the instructions of two or three tutors at least.

(2) Instructors should have skill in the art or method of teaching and practice of it.

(3) A good tutor will apply himself with diligence and concern.

(4) The tutor should take particular care that there be nothing in him which may be of ill example.

• Rules for the Learner

(1) The learner should attend with constancy and care on all the instructions of his tutor.

(2) A student should never satisfy himself with bare attendance.

(3) Let the learner endeavour to maintain an honourable opinion of his instructor.

(a) Pert young disciples soon fancy themselves wiser than those who teach them.

(b) Teachers and masters are not infallible.

(4) Authority of a teacher must not absolutely determine the judgment of his pupil.

Chapter 7: RULES OF IMPROVEMENT BY CONVERSATION

(1) It is a great happiness to be acquainted with persons wiser than ourselves.

(2) Waste not the time in trifle and impertinence.

(3) Lead *persons* into a discourse of the matters of their own peculiar province or profession.

(4) Confine not yourself always to one sort of company lest you should be confirmed and established in the same mistake by conversing with persons of the same sentiments.

(5) In mixed company among acquaintance and strangers, endeavour to learn something from all.

(6) Be not frighted nor provoked at opinions different from your own.

(7) Believe that it is possible to learn something from persons much below yourself.

(8) It is of considerable advantage, when we are pursuing any difficult point of knowledge, to have a society of ingenious correspondents at hand, to whom we may propose it.

(9) Let some one person take a book which may be agreeable to the whole company, and by common consent let him read in it.

(10) Whensoever it lies in your power to lead the conversation, let it be directed to some profitable point of knowledge or practice.

(11) Attend with sincere diligence.

(12) When a man gives his opinion in the plainest language of common sense do not presently imagine you shall gain nothing by his company.

(13) If you have not a clear idea of what is spoken, endeavour to obtain a clearer conception of it by a decent manner of inquiry.

(14) Represent what objection some persons would be ready to make against the sentiments of the speaker, without telling him you oppose.

(15) When you are forced to differ, represent how far you agree.

(16) Let your correspondent fairly finish his speech before you reply.

(17) Never remain in ignorance for want of asking.

(18) Be not too forward to determine any question with an infallible and peremptory sentence.

(19) Truth itself is in danger of being betrayed or lost, if there be no opposition made to a pretending talker.

    (a) A wise and a modest man may repel insolence with its own weapons.

    (b) A triumphant assurance hath sometimes supported gross falsehoods, and a whole company have been captivated to error till some man with equal assurance has rescued them.

(20) Be not fond of disputing every thing pro and con.

(21) Do not bring a warm party spirit into a conversation which is designed for mutual improvement in the search of truth.

(22) If you perceive a person unskilful in the matter of debate, lead him into a clearer knowledge of the subject.

(23) Take heed of affecting always to shine in company above the rest.

(24) Though you should not affect to flourish in a copious harangue and a diffusive style in company, yet neither should you rudely interrupt and reproach him that happens to use it: but reduce his sentiments into a more contracted form.

(25) Be not so ready to charge ignorance, prejudice, and mistake upon others as you are to suspect yourself of it.

(26) Banish utterly out of all conversation everything that tends to provoke passion or raise a fire in the blood.

(27) Whensoever any unhappy word shall arise in company command your tongue into silence. If this should not be sufficient, let a grave admonition, or a soft and gentle turn of wit give an occasion to stop the progress of his indecent fire.

(28) Inure yourself to a candid and obliging manner in all conversation.

(29) Choose such companions as may be capable of administering to your improvement.

(30) Nor is it every sober person of your acquaintance, no, nor every man of bright parts, or rich in learning, that is fit to engage in free conversation for the inquiry after truth if he lie under any of the following infirmities.

   (a) Exceedingly reserved.

   (b) Haughty and proud.

   (c) Positive and dogmatical.

   (d) Affects to outshine all the company.

   (e) Whiffling and unsteady turn of mind.

   (f) Fretful and peevish.

   (g) Affects wit on all occasions.

   (h) Crafty and cunning.

(31) You should watch against the working of these evil qualities in your breast.

(32) When you retire from company, converse with yourself in solitude.

    (a) If reason, decency, and civility have not been well observed amongst your associates, take notice of those defects for your own improvement.

    (b) By a review of irregularities you may learn to avoid follies.

• Disputes

    (1) When persons begin a debate, they should always take care that they are agreed in some general principles or propositions.

    (2) Let them search farther, and inquire how near they approach to each other's sentiments; and whatsoever propositions they agree in.

    (3) The question should be cleared from all doubtful terms and needless additions.

    (4) The precise point of inquiry should be distinctly fixed.

    (5) A resolute design of victory is the bane of all real improvement.

    (6) Enter the debate with a sincere design of yielding to reason, on which side soever it appears.

    (7) Watch narrowly in every dispute, that your opponent does not lead you unwarily to grant some principle of the proposition though it be far astray from the truth.

    (8) Make any such concession as may turn to your real advantage in maintaining the truth.

    (9) When you are engaged in dispute with a person of very different principles from yourself you may fairly make use of his own principles to shew him his mistake.

    (10) Great care must be taken, lest your debates break in upon your passions.

Chapter 8: STUDY OR MEDITATION

    (1) Learn betimes to distinguish between words and things.

    (2) Let not young students search out far above their reach.

(3) Nor yet let any student fright himself at every turn with insurmountable difficulties.

(4) In learning any new thing, there should be as little as possible first proposed to the mind at once.

(5) Engage not the mind in the intense pursuit of too many things at once.

(6) Where two or three sciences are pursued at the same time, if one of them be dry, let another be more entertaining and agreeable, to secure the mind from weariness.

(7) Keep the end always in your eye.

(8) Exert your care, skill, and diligence, about every subject and every question, in a just proportion to the importance of it.

    (a) Be very careful in gaining some general and fundamental truth.

    (b) In matters of practice we should be most careful to fix our end right.

    (c) Avoid such mistakes whose influence would be yet more extensive and injurious to others.

(9) Have a care lest some beloved notion, or some darling science, so far prevail over your mind as to give a sovereign tincture to all your other studies.

(10) Suffer not any beloved study to prejudice your mind so far in favour of it as to despise all other learning.

(11) Let every particular study have due and proper time assigned it.

(12) Do not apply yourself to any one study at one time longer than the mind is capable of giving a close attention to it without weariness or wandering.

(13) In the beginning of your application to any new subject, be not too uneasy under present difficulties that occur.

(14) Do not expect to arrive at certainty in every subject which you pursue.

(15) Endeavour to apply every speculative study to some practical use.

(16) Truth does not always depend upon the most convenient method.

Chapter 9: FIXING THE ATTENTION

(1) Get a good liking to the study or knowledge you would pursue.

(2) Sometimes we may make use of sensible things and corporeal images for the illustration of those notions which are more abstracted and intellectual.

(3) Apply yourself to those studies, and read those authors who draw out their subjects into a perpetual chain of connected reasonings.

(4) Do not choose your constant place of study by the finery of its prospects, or the most various and entertaining scenes of sensible things.

(5) Be not in too much haste to come to the determination of a difficult or important point.

(6) Have a care of indulging the more sensual passions and appetites of animal nature; they are great enemies to attention.

Chapter 10: ENLARGING THE CAPACITY OF THE MIND

* Noble Characteristics

(1) An ample and capacious mind which is ready to take in vast and sublime ideas without pain or difficulty.

(2) A mind *that* is free to receive new and strange ideas and propositions upon just evidence without any great surprise or aversion.

(3) An ability to receive many ideas at once without confusion.

* Rules

(1) Labour by all means to gain an attentive and patient temper of mind.

(2) Accustom yourself to clear and distinct ideas in every thing you think of.

(3) Use all diligence to acquire and treasure up a large store of ideas and notions.

(4) Entertain and lay up daily new ideas in a regular order.

(5) Observe a regular progressive method.

Chapter 11: IMPROVING THE MEMORY

- Rules

(1) *Pay* due attention and diligence to learn and know things which we would commit to our remembrance.

(2) Every thing which we learn should be conveyed to the understanding in the plainest expressions without any ambiguity.

  (a) Take heed that you do not take up with words instead of things, nor sounds instead of sentiments and ideas.

(3) Method and regularity in the things we commit to memory *is necessary.*

  (a) Whatsoever you would trust to your memory, let it be disposed in a proper method, connected well together and referred to distinct and particular heads or classes.

  (b) The mutual dependence of things on each other help the memory of both.

(4) A frequent review, and careful repetition of the things we would learn *will help fix them in the memory.*

  (a) Even when a person is hearing a lecture, he may give his thoughts leave now and then to step back so far as to recollect the several heads of it from the beginning.

  (b) If we would fix in the memory the discourses we hear, let us abstract them into brief compends, and review them often.

  (c) Do not plunge yourself into other businesses or studies, amusements or recreations, immediately after you have attended upon instruction.

  (d) Talking over the things which you have read with your companions is a most useful manner of review or repetition.

(5) Pleasure and delight in the things we learn give great assistance towards the remembrance of them.

(6) The memory of useful things may receive considerable aid if they are thrown into verse.

(7) When you would remember new things or words, endeavour to associate and connect them with some words or things which you have well known before.

(a) It is also by this association of ideas that we may better imprint any new idea upon the memory, by joining with it some circumstance wherein we first observed, heard, or learned it.

(b) Refer remembrance of names and things from our recollection of their likeness to other things.

(c) A new or strange idea may be fixed in the memory by considering its contrary or opposite.

(8) In such cases wherein it may be done, seek after a local memory, or a remembrance of what you have read by the side or page of where it is written or printed.

(9) Let every thing we desire to remember be legibly and distinctly written.

(a) Take notice of the advantage which the memory gains by schemes and tables.

(b) Once writing over what we design to remember, and giving due attention to what we write, will fix it more in the mind than reading it five times.

(10) It has sometimes been the practice of men to imprint names or sentences on their memory by taking the first letters of every word of that sentence, or of those names, and making a new word out of it.

Chapter 12: DETERMINING A QUESTION

- Considerations

  (1) Consider whether it be knowable at all.

  (2) Consider whether the matter be worthy of your inquiry.

  (3) Consider whether you have sufficient foundation or skill for the pursuit of it.

  (4) Consider whether the subject be any ways useful.

  (5) Consider what tendency it has to make you wiser and better.

- Preparing the Question

  (1) If it be dressed up and entangled in more words than is needful endeavour to reduce it to a greater simplicity and plainness.

(2) The stating a question with clearness goes a great way toward the answering of it.

(3) If the question relates to an axiom it should not be suddenly admitted or received.

> *(a)* It is not enough to say that it has been believed through many ages.

> *(b)* Nor is it enough to forbid any proposition the title of axiom, because it has been denied.

(4) While in search after truth keep up a just indifference to either side of the question.

> *(a)* Men without any industry or acquisition of their own inherit local truths.

> *(b)* If a man can bring his mind once to be positive and fierce for propositions whose evidence he hath never examined he will build all his opinions upon insufficient grounds.

- Determining the Question

  (1) Do not take up with partial examination, but turn your thoughts on all sides.

  (2) Take heed lest some darling notion be made a test of the truth or falsehood of all other propositions about the same subject.

  (3) Have a care of suddenly determining any one question on which the determination of any kindred or parallel cases will follow.

  (4) Raillery and wit were never made to answer our inquiries after truth, and to determine a question of rational controversy.

  (5) Let the force of argument alone influence your assent or dissent.

  (6) Sometimes a question is so large and extensive as ought not to be determined by a single argument or answer.

  (7) Take a full survey of the objections against it, as well as of the arguments for it, and see on which side the preponderation falls.

  (8) In matters of moment and importance, it is our duty indeed to seek after certain and conclusive arguments.

  (9) Many things which we believe with very different degrees of assent should be regulated according to the different degrees of evidence.

- Judging of Probabilities

  (1) That which agrees most with the constitution of nature carries the greatest probability in it.

  (2) That which is most conformable to the constant observations of men, is most likely to be true.

  (3) Where neither nature, nor observation, nor custom gives us any sufficient information, we may derive a probability from the attestation of wise and honest men.

- NOTES-